IDENTITY
solutions

IDENTITY *solutions*

HOW TO CREATE EFFECTIVE BRANDS WITH LETTERHEADS, LOGOS AND BUSINESS CARDS

HOW DESIGN BOOKS

www.howdesignbooks.com
HOW Design Books
Cincinnati, Ohio

CHERYL CULLEN & AMY SCHELL

About the Authors

Cheryl Dangel Cullen is a writer and public relations consultant specializing in the graphic arts industry. She is the author of more than 10 books from Rockport Publishers and has contributed articles to *HOW* Magazine, *Step-by-Step Graphics*, *Graphic Arts Monthly*, *American Printer*, *Printing Impressions* and *Package Printing & Converting*, among others. She is also the author of *The Art of Design* from HOW Design Books. Cullen Communications, a public relations firm she founded in 1992, provides public relations programs for clients in the graphic art, printing and paper industries. She lives near Chicago, Ilinois.

Amy Schell is an editor of HOW Design Books. She has worked on projects such as *The Art of Design*, *Graphically Speaking*, *Designing Websites for Every Audience*, and *Designers in Handcuffs*. She currently resides in Cincinnati, OH.

Other fine HOW Design Books are available from your local bookstore, art supply store or direct from the publisher.

07 06 05 04 03   5 4 3 2 1

Library of Congress Cataloging-in-Publication Data

Cullen, Cheryl Dangel.
    Identity solutions : how to create effective brands with letterheads, logos and business cards / Cheryl Cullen & Amy Schell.
            p. cm.
    Includes index.
    ISBN 1-58180-407-5 (hc : alk. paper)
     1. Business names. 2. Brand name products. 3. Corporate image. 4. Trademarks--Design. 5. Letterheads--Design. 7. Business cards--Design. I. Schell, Amy, 1979- II. Title.

HD69.B7C85 2003
658.8'27--dc21

Edited by Amy Schell
Editorial assistance by Eric Schwartzberg
Cover and interior design by Lisa Buchanan
Interior production by Kathy Bergstrom
Production coordinated by Sara Dumford
Photography by Tim Grondin

Dedication

To the designers whose boundless creativity continues to amaze me after all these years. Thank you. Your work makes writing a book like this feel like anything but work.

To my son Rhett, whose patience while I'm working at the computer is almost nearly perfect. Thank you.

CDC

SOLVE CHALLENGES CREATIVELY p. 10

1

UNCOVER SELF-PROMOTION SECRETS p. 98

3

FIND INNOVATIVE ANSWERS p. 46

2

ALANS • 11TH VISION • A MILLION MILES OF MOTIVATION • ACCORD INSURA
ARKER DÉCOR • AREA 51 INTERACTIVE • BALLET FOLKLORICO • BANDOLERO
HOTOGRAPHY • BINARY NET • BNIM ARCHITECTS • BY MINDY • CAFÉ TOLUCA
OMPANY • CHRISTINE CELIC • CHRISTOPHER SIMMONDS, ARCHITECT • CITY
ONNECTCARE • CONSTRUCTIONJOBS.COM • DAVE HEPLER, PIANIST • DIGITAL
ANPIMP • FETISH KINGS • FILMATERIA STUDIOS • FOR SOMEONE SPECIAL.
ATERING AND EVENT SERVICES • GLOW • GLY CONSTRUCTION • GRAPHIC RE

6

TABLE OF contents < < < < < < <

E • BROKERS • ADMINOVATION • AMERICAN RED CROSS, ATLANTA, GA • ANN
S • BARRETT RUDICH, PHOTOGRAPHER • BEAST OF THE EAST.NET • BIG DADD
NTRAL MICHIGAN PAPER • CHAPMAN SKATEBOARDS • CHOP'T CREATIVE SALA
WICHITA • CLADDAGH IRISH PUB • COLLABORATIVISIONS • COMPUTER CAFÉ
NET • DOGINC. • EL ZANJON • ELEMENTS IN DESIGN • ELEVATION • ERGONET
• FRENCHBREAD PRODUCTIONS • GHORMLEY CONSTRUCTION • GLADSTO
NSE • GREATLODGE.COM • GREEN TAGS • GSMR CONSULTING SERVICES • H
LIFE PRODUCTIONS • IZOOM • J RECORDS • JERRA TURNER • JEFFERSON

Introduction
Discover Designs that Work...

Identity design just may be one of the most important jobs you as a designer can tackle. The letterhead, logo, and business card designs you create are the cornerstones of branding. They are the face of your client's company. They sell your clients' products. They convey essential information. They present attitude. They are how every company begins to make a name for itself. The identity you create will determine how a company will be recognized now and in years to come.

Of course, everyone recognizes successful identity design when they see it. Kodak's famous yellow and black *K*, Nike's swoosh, McDonald's golden arches and IBM's bold letterforms are among the logos we recognize immediately. No explanation is necessary. These are identities that have stood the test of time.

But how, you may ask, do these great designs come about? They often start with just words spoken between a designer and a client. These words give birth to ideas that begin to take shape and are bounced back and forth. The ideas begin to appear on sketchpads and then computer screens. They are refined and tweaked and massaged until finally someone says, "A-ha! That's it!" And so an identity is born.

Of course, it doesn't go that smoothly every time. There are obstacles to overcome in every project. There are cranky clients. There are little bitty budgets. There are brain blocks that hide that one great idea. Sometimes it's difficult to find exactly the right solution. That's where we come in.

This book contains a spectacular collection of letterhead systems, logos, and business cards that have provided workable answers for the problems posed to them. A wide range of designers also share hints and tips that have helped them come up with the perfect solutions, so that you too can be inspired to find the perfect solution for your problem.

So jump in and take a look at all of the best new designs, browse the tips and advice offered by top designers, and get ready to be inspired.

SOLVE CHALLENGES
creatively

MindChisel

SHARON L. HAMBURGER
DESIGNER

SEVENTEENTH FLOOR
THREE GATEWAY CENTER
PITTSBURGH, PENNSYLVANIA
15222-1012 USA

DIRECT: 412.201.7005
MAIN: 412.288.9300
FACSIMILE: 412.281.8794
SHAMBURGER@MINDCHISEL.COM
WWW.MINDCHISEL.COM

fur

...cond Avenue Suite 2
Des Moines, Iowa 50313
phone
(515) 243-0718
(515) fax 243-0136

CHUNKY
Snazzletastic
ften times romantic
... cards

CREATE THAT FIRST IMPRESSION AND MAKE IT MEMORABLE. > > > > > > >

That's a tough assignment for anyone, but designers face it day after day when they are given the task of creating an identity. It's hard to put a puzzle together when you're not sure what all the pieces look like. You have to figure out what the client wants. You have to figure out what style will best communicate with the audience. You have to figure out the colors, the fonts, the placement of elements, and the feel of the piece. In addition, an identity makes a personal statement, and this fact alone can make it difficult for clients to choose a focus and provide a direction.

Compounding the puzzle even more is the longevity required of an identity. Clients need to be happy with the result the designer delivers because they will have to live with it for a long time. In addition, there may be budget constraints, or creative limits, or strict guidelines you have to follow to create a workable identity for your client. How do these pieces fit in?

The designs on the following pages show how some designers overcame these problems and many more. They strike a chord at first glance and make an indelible impression. Many of them may look like they were designed with no set budget and no creative constraints, and yet they were. Take a look at the designs and read how these top-notch designers put their own puzzle pieces together to create truly revolutionary designs.

Pearl Restaurant Identity

Studio: [i]e design, Los Angeles
Art Director: Marcie Carson
Designers: Marcie Carson, Cya Nelson
Client: MGM Grand, Las Vegas
Paper: Amori Gmund Ever Cream
Colors: four-color process plus two
    match colors
Font: Futura, Grand Central Light
Special Techniques: menu—silver foil;
    letterhead—tint varnish

A new restaurant was opening at Las Vegas' MGM Grand and no one knew what kind of restaurant it would be—let alone its name. Competing against other firms for the project, [i]e design created four menu comps with the name *Zen* before they were awarded the project along with a final decision on the name—*Pearl*.

"The logo design was driven by the client," says Alli Neiman, [i]e design. "They wanted a Chinese symbol that represented a woman's name—Pearl." Designers decided to combine a modern font, Futura, alongside the ancient symbol to create a visual metaphor for an authentic yet stylish and contemporary Chinese restaurant.

The designers chose the paper stock for its textural feel and scaly, fish-skin-like appearance, perfect for a Chinese seafood restaurant. The final system has a balanced design that is clean, modern and functional enough for everyday handling.

TIP

An identity system is an extension of the logo. Create an environment for the logo to deliver its message, but don't try too hard for visual harmony. A successful identity thrives on tension.

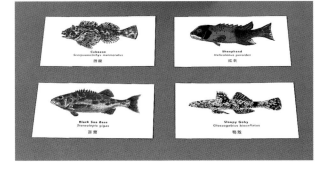

Witness Productions Identity

Studio: Chen Design Associates
Art Director: Joshua C. Chen
Designer: Max Spector
Client: Witness Productions
Paper: Strathmore Pure Cotton
Colors: one match color
Print Run: 2,000 of each
Cost Per Unit: $1.50
Special Techniques: Custom converted envelopes;
    rubber-stamping for second color

As soon as Witness Productions, a documentary film company, awarded Chen Design Associates the job of creating its identity, designers immediately considered basing it on the look of an official document—in particular, a passport. A passport "would allow these documentary makers to travel the world to 'give sight and sound to people whose presence is virtually forgotten,'" says Joshua Chen, quoting from the client's brief.

Working with a tight budget, Chen Design Associates created a system that communicates the significance of Witness Productions' work on a one-color budget. "We met that challenge by printing on press in one color, and adding a second color using a rubber stamp, which tied in well with the passport concept."

TIP

Rubber stamps can customize a letterhead design and add additional color without adding to the cost.

Dave Hepler Identity

Studio: Lodge Design Co.
Designer: Eric Kass
Client: Dave Hepler
Paper: letterhead—French Construction Cement
    Green; *business card*—French Construction Char-
    coal Brown; *envelope*—French Construction Safe-
    ty Orange
Print Run: 500
Cost: $1,000 for whole system
Special Technique: Letterpress printing

Dave Hepler, a jazz pianist, needed a professional system that would identify him when he plays local gigs and promotes his newest CD to record labels and jazz festivals worldwide. It also needed to be flexible enough to work on packaging. "The improvisational, yet symmetrically structured mark occurs simultaneously with the pianist's name and number," says Eric Kass. "The word 'pianist' falls against the rectangle, with parentheses resonating from it—as if it were a hammer hitting the string as a note is pounded on the key. The metallic silver artwork seems to change volume as it appears on varying tones of paper—quieter on the darker stocks, louder on the lighter stocks."

Why print the pieces on a letterpress? "It is more personal and [conveys a] crafted feeling matching the artist's approach to music," explains Kass.

The challenge with this project—as in many identity systems—was the limited budget. "Letterpress printing in one color can create a very unique appearance for a surprisingly affordable price," says Kass.

TIP

If you're on a tight budget, consider letterpress printing. It provides a very tactile, handcrafted appearance without the cost. You can also use the same letterpress block on all pieces in an identity system to eliminate the cost of producing a separate block for each item.

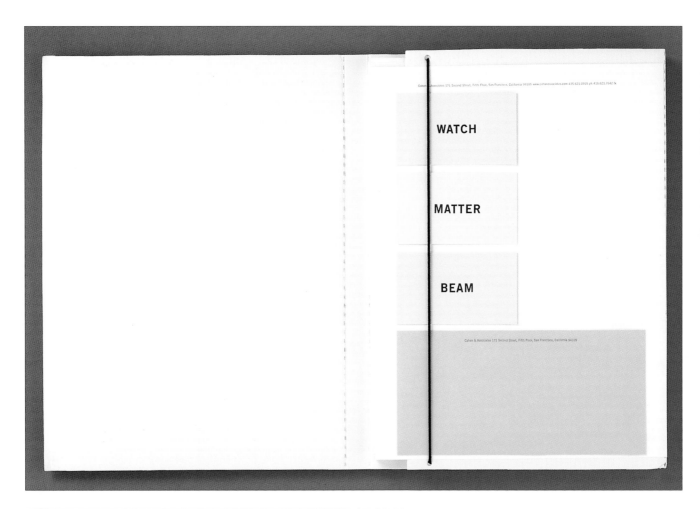

IRON Identity

Studio: Cahan & Associates
Art Director: Bill Cahan
Designers: Bob Dinetz, Kevin Roberson
Colors: one match color
Print Run: 25,000
Special Technique: Letterpress printing

"The way we look at ourselves is in service of our clients," says Kevin Roberson, designer. "Our identity is almost irrelevant compared to our work." Therefore, designers decided to go with a very minimalist look for their self promotion.

The challenge, according to Roberson, was to come up with a minimal solution that retained "just enough" personality. The solution incorporates subtle changes of color, printing techniques and words into the identity. Words were chosen to be deliberately innocuous so as to pique curiosity.

TIP

Minimalism does not have to be boring. Make sure you have a strong concept, then execute it with as few lines as possible.

MindChisel Identity

Studio: Brady Communications
Art Directors: Jim Brady, Jim Bolander
Designer: Jim Bolander
Client: MindChisel
Paper: Neenah Classic Crest Brilliant
White
Colors: three match colors
Print Run: letterhead and envelope—
1,000; *business cards*—750
Cost Per Unit: letterhead—$.37; enve-
lope—$.26; business cards—$2.05

Look at this system and what do you notice first? The innovative business cards.

"These thought-provoking cards were developed to stand out from standard business cards," says Jim Bolander, one of the art directors on the project. "Incorporating sayings on the back—which range from inspirational to challenging to humorous—added a unique and memorable element."

Indeed, the cards are eye-catching and worth the extra expense they added to the budget. The address side was printed in two colors, while names and personal information are imprinted on separate press runs as needed.

"Decide what your identity system should say about the client. For instance, 'We are young, fun and cool to work for' or 'We are a big, serious company that you can trust.'"

JIM BOLANDER

Jebra Turner Identity

Studio: Dotzero Design
Art Directors/Designers: Karen Wippich, Jon Wippich
Client: Jebra Turner
Paper: Classic Columns Solar White
Printing: Ink-jet

On a budget? Consider designing the job for ink-jet printing and hand-assembly. That's what Dotzero Design did for Jebra Turner, who prints out stickers for her letterhead system as needed and as time permits, then assembles the stickers onto the paper stock by hand. "This way, there is no big printing cost and we were able to design four color schemes for her," says Jon Wippich, art director.

The client wanted a system that she could customize to the recipient. Originally, she envisioned adding the customized element through different paper stocks, but then she saw Dotzero's varying logo designs.

"Once the client saw the logo comps, she wondered if we could find a way for her to use a few of them," says Wippich. They settled on using a light bulb as the common mark, and putting various icons within the light bulb for variety.

"An identity should embody the attitude of the product, service or company and convey a message of who or what they are. This goes for font choices as well as mark design and other graphics. A font and look should be designed because it is a good fit, not just because it is a trend."

JON WIPPICH

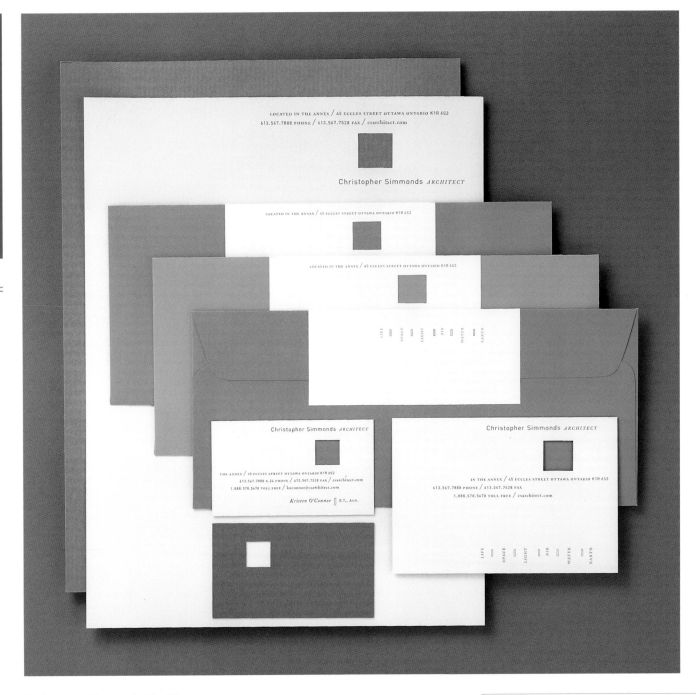

Christopher Simmonds Identity

Studio: Iridium, a design agency
Art Directors: Jean-Luc Denat, Mario L'Écuyer
Designer: Mario L'Écuyer
Client: Christopher Simmonds, Architect
Paper: Gilbert Voice, French Papers Construction
Colors: 2 match colors
Size: 4³/₄" x 3¹/₄" (12 cm x 8.5 cm)
Print Run: 2,000
Special Techniques: Square die cut on each item; different size stickers for envelopes

This architectural firm designs places open to life and nature, so designers decided to create an identity that was minimalist and holistic in form, yet spiritual in content.

At the cornerstone of the identity is a simple square die cut. Ask the designers why the system works and they credit the simple square. "The die-cut technique accomplished its mission and fueled curiosity and interesting conversations," says Mario L'Écuyer, art director.

> "In view of the client's philosophy and practice, opening the tactile surface of the various items with square windows reflects on the firm's attachment to Eastern elementalism—where earth, water, fire, and air co-exist at equilibrium in the shape of a square—and eventually, liberate the Shi, the earth energy in Feng Shui."
>
> MARIO L'ÉCUYER

Rick Ball | sales | rick@srws.com

444 Via El Centro
Oceanside, CA 92054
F 760.721.3605
P 760.721.3664 ▶

the real feel of rock. | www.srws.com ▶

Solid Rock Identity

Studio: Parker White
Art Directors: Cindy White, Dylan Jones
Designer: Cindy White
Client: Solid Rock Wall Systems
Paper: Sundance Ultra White 70 lb. text and 110 lb. cover
Colors: two match colors
Print Run: 8,500
Cost Per Unit: $.28

Solid Rock Wall Systems makes and engineers climbing walls for military training, gyms, and recreational theme parks. With the desire to update its look for a more modern appearance, the firm turned to Parker White. Using a bold triangle to represent the wall, designers added an abstract image of a climber.

Designers were careful to present an image that's versatile enough to represent all the client's endeavors—not only its capabilities to manufacture climbing walls for gyms. "The abstract illustration of the climber helps do this because it doesn't pigeonhole them into one market," says Dylan Jones, art director.

TIP

To save money, print business cards as blank shells so that they can be customized easily for new hires with a simple one-color printing.

Three Forty Four Design Logo

Studio: Three Forty Four Design
Art Director/Designer: Stefan Bucher

Chop't Salad Logo

Studio: Platinum Design, Inc.
Art Director: Vickie Peslak
Designers: Kelly Hogg, Julie Nathon
Client: Chop't Creative Salad
    Company, a food service company
Colors: four-color process

Maison Ray Logo

Studio: Headwerk, LLC
Art Director/Designer: Erik Weber
Client: Maison Ray, a multi-line
    designer clothing showroom
Colors: metallic PMS 8601, PMS 5025

Milestone Logo

Studio: X Design Company
Art Director: Alex Valderrama
Designers: Alex Valderrama,
    Jen Dahlen
Client: Milestone Construction
    Management

Wisconsin Independent Books Logo

Studio: BL_NK
Art Director/Designer: Dave Blank
Client: Wisconsin Independent Books,
    an independent book publisher

METRO®

KLŌN KLŌN

She LIKES DVDs.COM

Metro Logo

Studio: Turner Duckworth
Art Directors: David Turner, Bruce Duckworth
Designers: Allen Raulet, Sarah Moffat
Client: Metro Furniture Company, a high-end office furniture design and manufacturing company

Klon Film Logo

Studio: Epoxy Communication, Inc.
Art Director/Designer: George Fok
Client: Klon Film Company, a production company owned by twin brothers

Lunchclub.net Logo

Studio: Catapult Strategic Design
Art Director/Designer: Peter Jones
Client: Lunchclub.net, a free internet service that provides daily lunch discounts via email

Moulin Groove Logo

Studio: Greteman Group
Art Directors: James Strange, Sonia Greteman
Designer: James Strange
Client: Moulin Groove, a fundraising event held by ConnectCare, an AIDS service organization

She Likes DVDs Logo

Studio: Buchanan Design
Art Director/Designer: Lisa Buchanan
Client: SheLikesDVDs.com, an entertainment web site

A Million Miles of Motivation Identity

Studio: McArtor Design
Art Director/Designer: Jason McArtor
Client: Rob Wilson, A Million Miles of Motivation
Paper: French Construction Whitewash
Colors: four-color process plus one match and one
letterpress (gold) on business card
Print Run: letterhead—6,000; *business card*—1,000;
stickers—3,000
Special Technique: Use of stickers

"I want my picture on my materials," was the
mandate from Rob Wilson, a motivational speaker
who believes that above all, his identity materials
need to sell him.

"We were immediately faced with the problem
of working a photograph into a letterhead and
business card system," says Jason McArtor, art
director. "The last thing we wanted to do was drop
a head shot into a box on the front of a glossy
four-color business card."

The solution was to use a full body action
shot, which showcased the client's personality
and the energy he brings to his work. "We know
the system has worked because, almost a year
later, Rob still hears 'cool card' from his clients,"
explains McArtor.

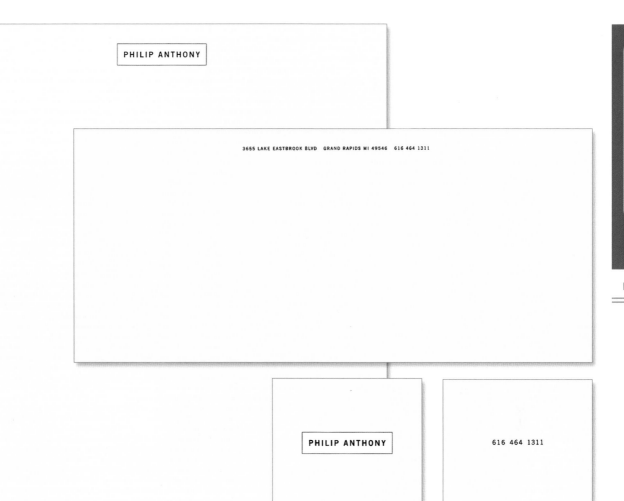

Philip Anthony Identity

Studio: BBK Studio
Art Directors: Kevin Budelmann, Yang Kim
Designer: Alison Popp
Client: Philip Anthony Salon & Spa
Paper: Beckett Concept Radiance White, 130 lb. cover
Colors: two match colors plus coating
Print Run: 1,000 each of 12 names; 28,000 blanks
Special Technique: Embossing

Philip Anthony Salon & Spa needed an identity that conveyed the upscale nature of its work. "We wanted the identity system to be modern yet have a classical feel," says Kevin Budelmann, art director. "We wanted a tactile, emotive solution that would give the business cards a higher-quality presence."

Designers had hoped to engrave the pieces, but the budget was limited so they opted for embossing instead.

 TIP

Specialty printing techniques such as foil stamping, engraving, embossing, and thermography don't always have to break the budget. Find out how costs compare and you may be surprised at the affordability of mixing and matching these techniques.

Ballet Folklorico Identity

Studio: Dennard, Lacey & Associates
Art Director: Bob Dennard
Designers: Keith Carroll, James Lacey
Client: Anita N. Martinez—Ballet Folklorico
Paper: Gilbert Paper Neu Tech
Colors: one match color
Print Run: 1,500
Special Technique: Die cut on inside pocket

Designers created this identity to represent the many aspects of the Ballet Folklorico, from Mayan tribal dance to traditional Hispanic dance. Using a simple one-color design, the choice of color and ethnic imagery—including the two dancing figures—communicates the organization's diversity. The die cuts on the inside pockets of the folder mirror the shapes of the figures depicted on the business card.

"Start with the name. Make sure the mark is unique to the name. If you have no choice in the name and it isn't particularly strong to begin with, make sure the mark is graphically strong and something hard to forget."

JAMES LACEY

GSMR Identity

Studio: Pacifico Integrated Marketing
    Communications
Art Director: Boyd Tveit
Designer: Julie Mount
Client: GSMR Consulting Services
Paper: Fox River Select Circa Script Natural Laid Finish
    28 lb. and 80 lb.
Colors: four match colors
Print Run: 1,000
Special Techniques: Letterpress printing; embossing
    of the crest

"The client wanted an upscale look and lives in Pebble Beach, California, which has a strong Spanish influence," explains Boyd Tveit, creative director. "This determined the color scheme. In addition, the business is co-owned by four in-laws, all of whom are of Scottish descent, hence the crest and initials."

So much came easily to this design that there was bound to be a challenge on press—and there was. It wasn't easy achieving accurate registration of the crest hairline and the embossing. "Originally, the idea was to emboss just the crest, but the hairline required such exacting standards that registration was a problem," recalls Tveit. "The printer came up with the idea of debossing the beige square surrounding the crest, creating the visual illusion of an embossed crest. Don't ask me why, but it worked."

> **TIP**
>
> *Query the client about their hobbies, interests, family, etc. You never know where you'll find inspiration for a logo, a color palette, or a typeface.*

> *"Design simply. Execute flawlessly. And remember to consider the tactile value of the end product. Those things alone can produce memorable identity programs."*
>
> BOYD TVEIT

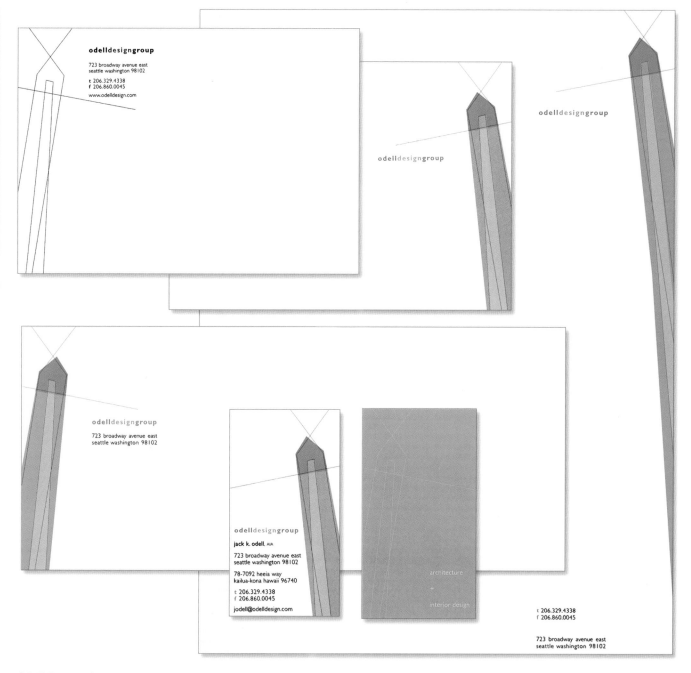

Odell Design Group Identity

Studio: Monster Design
Art Directors: Hannah Wygal, Theresa Veranth
Designer: Hannah Wygal
Client: Odell Design Group
Paper: Mohawk Superfine
Colors: two match colors

The Odell Design Group, an architectural firm in search of a new identity, tapped Monster Design for help. Once on board, designers decided to illustrate the idea of elevating a home to a higher level, while also highlighting the firm's move to a new studio. Designers accomplished this with thin, structural lines, which they used to convey the linear quality of architecture. By skewing the lines and placing some colors outside the form, they added an artistic flair to the identity, which in turn communicates the architectural firm's unique design capabilities.

"Bending the rules on this logo—making it less of a freestanding element and more of a design that really works with the page— was our way of making a statement about our identity. We wanted to emphasize the creative nature of the Odell Design Group. This logo reflects the mindset of an archi- tect—someone who conceptualizes using the entire spatial plane."

HANNAH WYGAL

Katie McCall Business Cards

Studio: Know Name Design
Art Director/Designer: Jason Burton
Client: Katie McCall
Paper: Potlatch McCoy Silk 120 lb. cover
Colors: 2 over 2 plus varnish
Size: $1^3/_4$" x $3^1/_2$" (3 cm x 9 cm)
Print Run: 1,000
Cost Per Unit: $.73

These cards were built around the personality of Katie McCall, a bright and cheery on-camera and voice talent professional. They are skinnier than traditionally sized cards and feature a stand-out logo on one side. "We attempted several color combinations, and the orange and purple really shouts, 'Katie!' The voice bubble was a given. It is to the point, clever, and an icon that we all recognize," says Jason Burton, art director.

Filmateria Business Cards

Studio: Terry Marks Design
Art Director: Terry Marks
Designers: Terry Marks, Josh Michels
Client: Filmateria Studios
Paper: Cougar Opaque Uncoated 100 lb. cover
Colors: four-color process
Print Run: 400

Illustrations that echo 1940s film posters are the perfect images for this film/video company's calling cards, which have die cuts so the business card itself resembles a movie ticket.

Technical Treeworks Business Cards

Studio: Catapult Strategic Design
Art Director/Designer: Peter Jones
Client: Technical Treeworks
Colors: two match colors
Size: $2^3/_8$" (6 cm)
Print Run: 500

Leaves were the inspiration for this business card, made for a company that diagnoses, trims and treats sick and healthy trees. "But this firm isn't your standard tree doctor; they are high-tech arborists, so the card's shape is rounded to resemble a high-tech leaf," says Peter Jones, art director. "They only had enough money for a logo and a card, so the card had to be full of impact. We solved that with the unique shape."

Youth Culture Group Identity

Studio: Amoeba Corp.
Art Director: Michael Kelar
Designer: Jason Darbyson
Client: Youth Culture Group
Paper: Beckett Expression Super Smooth
Colors: four-color process both sides, plus spot UV on
kit folder
Special Techniques: A sticker system for four divisions
rather than four separate kit folders; die cut on
business cards and kit folder

The Youth Culture Group, developer of television
programming for young people, publisher of teen-
focused magazines and provider of an array of

services for Canadian youth, needed an identity
as diverse as its services without diluting its
brand equity. Moreover, it had to be exciting, pro-
gressive, and youthful to appeal to its teen audience while not offending or confusing its
secondary audience—business executives.

Rather than produce four separate kit folders,
designers created a visual sticker system to customize each of the organizations four divisions.
As such, the sub-brands are tied together under a
consistent family identity while maintaining an
element of a separate identity for each. Michael
Kelar, art director, describes the look as "technology meets a bowl of fruit loops."

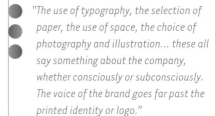

*"The use of typography, the selection of
paper, the use of space, the choice of
photography and illustration… these all
say something about the company,
whether consciously or subconsciously.
The voice of the brand goes far past the
printed identity or logo."*

MICHAEL KELAR

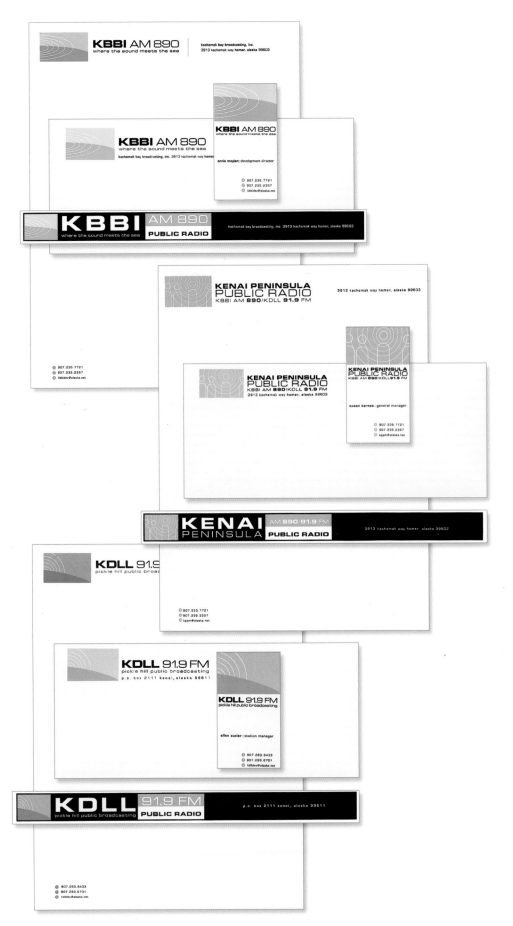

Kachemak Bay Radio Stations' Identity

Studio: Michael Lotenero Illustration
     and Design
Art Director/Designer: Michael Lotenero
Client: Kachemak Bay Broadcasting
Paper: Mohawk Superfine Ultra Smooth
Colors: three match colors
Print Run: 1,000

The client, a public radio station, needed consistent identities for each of its three public broadcasting counterparts. Each station needed a logo to reflect its individual name, yet it needed to be uniform with the other two. Designer/illustrator Michael Lotenero accomplished this by using sound waves alongside each station's tag line.

KBBI, "where the sound meets the sea," utilizes the blue of the water for its background. KDLL, Pickle Hill Public Broadcasting, has sound waves over a green hilltop. And lastly, KPPR's identity features sound waves on an orange background, which balances the green and the blue.

"Fancy folds and die cuts are fun, but sometimes clients just need a solid card, envelope and letterhead. What makes this one work is its simplicity. The process was very simple and direct. Everyone got what they wanted out of this one, and that makes me happy."

MICHAEL LOTENERO

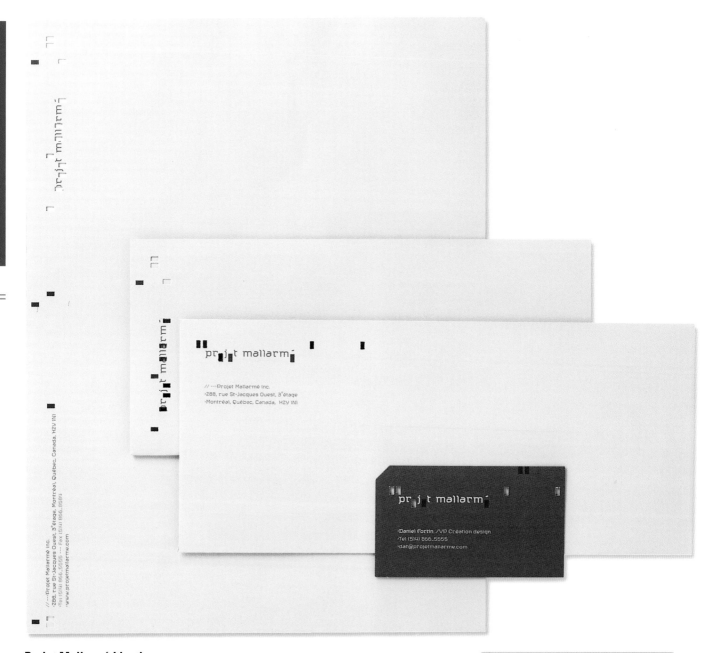

Projet Mallarmé Identity

Studio: Époxy Communication, Inc.
Creative Directors: Daniel Fortin, George Fok
Art Directors: Eric Dubois, Jean Christophe Yacono
Designer: Eric Dubois

Projet Mallarmé creates and produces multimedia projects, including CDs, DVD-ROMs and Internet-based e-commerce solutions. In need of a new identity that conveyed the high-tech nature of its business, it called upon Époxy for help.

"Projet" represents the constant effort to create new forms of communication. "Mallarmé" is the name of a French poet, which reflects the cultural and artistic nature of the company. "Since the poet is famous for his nonlinear poetry, he acts as a symbol…for the language of new medias," explains Eric Dubois, art director and designer on the project. From a technical aspect, designers decided to associate the company with a punch card, which also works as a visual metaphor for the non-linear poetry of Mallarmé.

As a result, holes similar to punch card holes are cut into the system. Designers created a special typeface based on Courier, which spells out only a portion of the client's name. When the letterhead is folded in thirds, the entire company name is revealed through the punched holes as though in code. The missing characters that show through are cleverly printed on the reverse side of the paper.

TIP

If the exact font you want doesn't exist, make one. Stylize an existing font to create the look you're after.

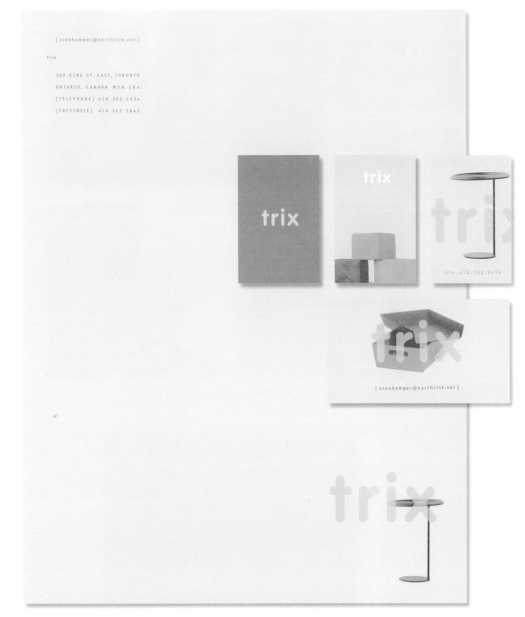

Trix Identity

Studio: Bløk Design
Art Director: Vanessa Eckstein
Designer: Stephanie Yung
Client: Trix
Paper: Benefit
Colors: three match colors
Print Run: 3,000

"The stationery system is a simple expression of the elements and designs which make Trix unique," says Vanessa Eckstein, art director. Her client, Trix, manufactures a designed line of high quality leather furniture and accessories.

The designer used a warm palette that reflects the warmth of materials inherent in Trix's product line and a stock with "more tooth" was chosen to reflect the tactile qualities of the leather products. Simple photography—also reproduced in warm tones—drives home the message by showing exactly how different this company's products are.

TIP

Consider the type of photography and the texture of the paper you want to use. Use these subtle elements to enhance or emphasize a certain idea in your piece.

Les Piafs Business Card

Studio: Belyea
Art Director: Patricia Belyea
Designers: Kelli Lewis, Naomi Murphy
Client: Les Piafs
Paper: Neenah Classic Crest 130 lb. cover
Colors: Fluorescent process over black, plus one
    match color
Print Run: 5,000 each of 4

Les Piafs, a high-end vintage lifestyle boutique, boasts cards that feature a complex tabletop composition of vintage artifacts photographed from above. The client, a collector of quirky and unique treasures, liked the idea of creating original art and pulled the items together from her own collection. In addition to using the photo collages on the business cards, the designers also used it on a series of promotional postcards and in-store price tags, making the artwork extremely cost-efficient.

Barrett Rudich Business Card

Studio: Jeff Fisher LogoMotives
Art Director/Designer: Jeff Fisher
Client: Barrett Rudich
Colors: Black foil, gray ink
Size: 2" x 3¹/₈" (5 cm x 8.3 cm)
Print Run: 1,000

This client, a professional photographer, wanted an identity that reflected his specialty—black and white photography—so he requested a black-on-black business card. The problem was convincing a printer that black foil on black paper would work.

"Then we threw embossing into the mix," recalls Jeff Fisher, art director. "I had previously used clear foils and varnishes to produce similar effects and used those examples to attempt to explain the concept. Finally an embossing house did a sample, and the project was set to go."

It's a Wonderful Life Business Card

Studio: Thumbnail Creative Group
Art Directors: Rik Klingle, Judith Austin
Designer: Valerie Turnbull
Client: It's a Wonderful Life Productions, Inc.
Paper: Mohawk Vellum
Colors: two match colors
Print Run: 5,000
Cost Per Unit: $.40

It's a Wonderful Life is a media production company that specializes in positive, community-oriented projects. This fact is perfectly reflected in its business card, with the choice of typeface and the icon of a business man jumping in the air and clicking his heels together. Designers wanted to avoid traditional media images and cleanly steered clear of them in favor of this vintage image.

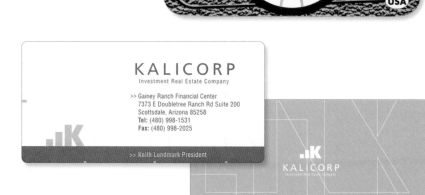

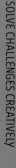
Celic Business Card

Studio: Pomeroy Dakota
Art Director: Christine Celic, Eric Strohl
Paper: French Dur-o-Tone
Colors: three match colors

A special duplex stock was created by hand for this business card. It incurred the only cost in an overall system, which was printed and assembled as needed in the studio.

By Mindy Greetings Business Card

Studio: Digital Slant
Art Director: Cami Boehme
Designer: Jeff Norgord
Client: By Mindy
Paper: Standard Chipboard
Colors: one match color
Print Run: 1,000
Cost Per Unit: $.11

This budget business card uses only one color and is printed on scrap paper, then torn by hand to save even more money, resulting in a card that cost just eleven cents a piece. In addition to being cost-cutting, it delivers a distinct message for this maker of handcrafted greeting cards. The logo appears to be handwritten, and the entire presentation is personal and custom crafted.

Big Daddy Business Card

Studio: Sayles Graphic Design
Art Director/Designer: John Sayles
Client: Big Daddy Photography
Paper: Mohawk Navajo
Colors: three match colors
Print Run: 2,000

Photographer Roger Kennedy wanted an unusual identity for his studio and got what he asked for in this business card, which is die-cut in the shape of a camera. The whole approach is humorous and memorable.

Kalicorp Business Card

Studio: SDZYNE
Art Director/Designer: Spencer Walters
Client: Kalicorp Investment Real Estate Company
Colors: two match colors
Print Run: 1,000
Cost Per Unit: $1.80

"The client is young and wanted something cool," says Spencer Walters, art director, "but he realized his audience wanted something sound. So we agreed to do a cool pattern for the back of the system but make the information side 'sound' by using a lot of space and readable type, as well as two hues of green to symbolize money."

Anne Parker Decor Identity

Studio: Lloyds Graphic Design and
      Communication
Art Director/Designer: Alexander Lloyd
Client: Anne Parker
Paper: Mataura Falls By BT Bau
Colors: four-color process
Print Run: 500

This system leaves little doubt that this letterhead is about interior design. It works because it leaves the recipient with the feeling that it is a custom job—as evidenced by the mock job numbers printed in random order vertically down the edge of each piece.

The challenge for this designer was steering clear of usual interior design clichés—furniture illustrations and brushstrokes. Instead, art director Alexander Lloyd made colorful swatches the principal icon.

Why does it work? "Because of the utilitarian look and feel of the logo/stationery, nothing glitzy or ostentatious," says Lloyd. "Practical simplicity is encapsulated in the job numbers, staples, and swatch icons, which use different colors across all stationery items for a feeling of individuality."

"Wherever possible, keep the concept and corresponding design as simple as possible. It has been said many times before; the key to effective identities is simplicity. Don't allow a great concept to become diluted or lost in pretty pictures and technique."

ALEXANDER LLOYD

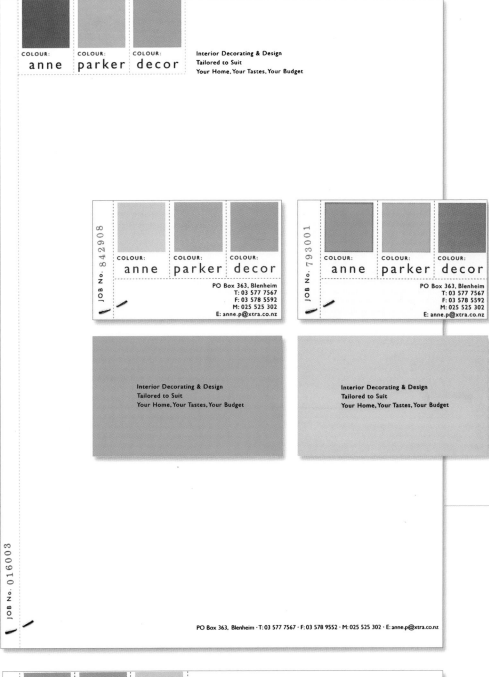

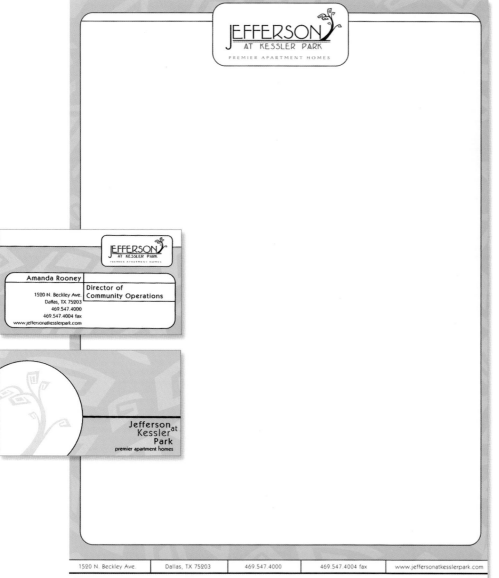

Jefferson at Kessler Park Identity

Studio: VWA Group
Art Director: Rhonda Warren
Designers: Jill Maddux, Dana Beeney
Client: TPI
Paper: Mohawk Options
Colors: two match colors
Print Run: 2,500
Special Technique: Envelope was printed, then converted

TPI offers luxury apartment rentals called Jefferson at Kessler Park, which has mission-style architecture and is located in an historic neighborhood of Dallas, Texas. Designers chose a crisp typeface and a spring-like color palette for an uplifting feeling that fit the location. The pattern used in the background gives a feeling of texture and projects a timeless, classic aura.

> "You can do a lot with one or two colors if you practice good design and innovation."
>
> RHONDA WARREN

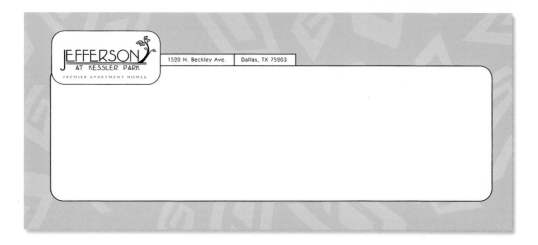

Midwest Sports Identity

Studio: McArtor Design
Art Director/Designer: Jason McArtor
Client: Midwest Sports Syndicators
Paper: French Frostone Flurry
Colors: two match colors
Print Run: 1,000
Cost Per Unit: $1.00

"'Classic' and 'traditional' were the key words for this system," says Jason McArtor of the letterhead he designed for Midwest Sports Syndicators, a syndicator of sports radio programming. "We wanted the design to suggest something sporty, but the direction needed to be Ivy League."

McArtor explains that this refined system allowed his client to compete with other high-profile companies, something that probably wouldn't have happened if the client had created the identity himself, as he initially wanted to.

TIP

Investigate nontraditional materials, such as metal, rubber, or plastic to help your client stand out from their competition.

Urban Fare Identity

Studio: Karacters Design Group
Creative Director: Maria Kennedy
Art Director/Designer: Matthew Clark
Client: Urban Fare
Paper: Navajo
Colors: four-color process plus two
    match colors

Designer Matthew Clark created this identity by breaking his client's name, Urban Fare, into its key elements—food and the city. Doing so inspired him to use an industrial-age logo and to combine it with the color palette of the city—stone and metal. It is this combination that he used throughout the corporate identity, collateral materials, and retail and environmental identity.

"The system had to defy the traditional supermarket experience and celebrate gourmet food in an urban setting," says Clark. "First came the name with its straightforward dichotomy; then the logo with its visual metaphor and nod to a chic location; then the signage and retail identity embracing urban materials and sensual food imagery. The stationery was easy."

"Getting noticed is easy. Everybody tries to get noticed, but being interesting enough to be remembered and to be loved is hard. Be smart. Don't try to be too cool. And quit shouting. It's annoying."

MATTHEW CLARK

ANYBODY WHO
HATES DOGS AND
LOVES WHISKY
CAN'T BE
ALL THAT BAD

W.C. FIELDS

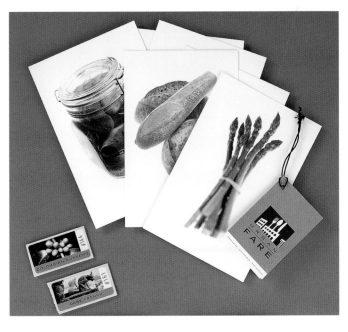

Lifestyles Logo

Studio: Ideograma
Art Director: Juan Carlos Fernández
Designer: Susanne Ortiz
Client: Iser, a furniture store

2 Trees Design Logo

Studio: 2 Trees Design
Art Director/Designer: Jacob Zwei-
  bohmer

Melissa & Company Logo

Studio: Headwerk, LLC
Art Director/Designer: Erik Weber
Client: Melissa & Company Salon, a
  full service salon and day spa
Colors: PMS 504, PMS 187

Good Paper Logo

Studio: BBK Studio
Art Director/Designer: Yang Kim
Client: Central Michigan Paper, a
  paper distributor
Colors: two match colors

UndeRadar Logo

Studio: Ken Rabe, Graphic Designer
Art Directors: Ken Rabe, Bill Gordon
Designer: Ken Rabe
Client: UndeRadar Records
Colors: two match colors

iProTalk

Wells Fargo Women's Open Logo

Studio: X Design Company
Art Director/Designer: Alex Valderrama
Client: Wells Fargo golf tournament

Dapzury Valenzuela Logo

Studio: Dapzury Valenzuela
Art Director/Designer: Dapzury
Valenzuela
Colors: PMS 5767, PMS 458, PMS 653,
PMS 116

Pinetree Campgrounds Logo

Studio: dpainter_dsgns
Art Director/Designer: Donald Painter
Client: National Park System

iProTalk Logo

Studio: Cahan & Associates
Art Director: Bill Cahan
Designer: Michael Braley
Client: iProTalk, Inc., an online
community resource center

The American Dream

Studio: Louviere & Vanessa
Art Director/Designer: Jeff Louviere
Client: The American Dream client, a
guy in New Orleans who creates
public art about life and politics

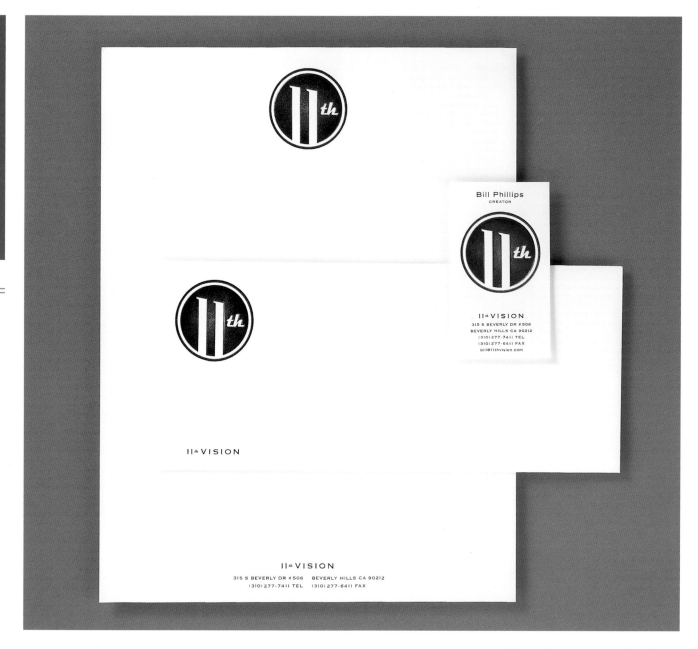

11th Vision Identity

Studio: Digital Soup
Art Director/Designer: Pash
Client: 11th Vision
Paper: Crane's Crest and Crane's Cover
Print Run: business cards—1,000 each of three; *letterhead*—2,000
Special Techniques: It was a four-step process: solid silver foil in the shape of the logo was laid down; duotone was created and two-color offset printed on top of the foil; the logo was embossed; contact information was engraved

11th Vision, a media company that creates uplifting, empowering education books, audio tapes, CDs, newsletters and more, came to Digital Soup in need of a new identity that incorporated the numeral eleven. Digital Soup went to work on the project and showed the client a glowing, shiny, three-dimensional version of the logo on screen. They loved it.

Now the problem set in. The client wanted this version of the logo replicated on Crane's 100% cotton paper, which they chose for their stationery system. "How exactly does one create something glowing, shiny, and 3-D on cotton paper?" Pash remembers asking.

To solve the problem, Pash turned to a specialty printer for help. After much brainstorming and six weeks of experimentation, the team was able to finalize the production details and the look the client wanted was achieved.

"We must remember that we are trying to visually represent something that a client will often have trouble putting into words. We are detectives, image specialists, and narrators, even psychologists. We must not only help our clients promote themselves the 'right' way, but we must also help them see themselves the way that others see them."

PASH

For Someone Special Identity

Studio: Karacters Design Group
Art Directors: Matthew Clark, Nancy Wu
Designer: Nancy Wu
Client: ForSomeoneSpecial.com
Paper: Mohawk Superfine
Colors: four match colors
Print Run: business cards—500 each of 10 with 10,000
blanks; *letterhead*—1,000 printed, 1,000 blank;
#10 envelopes and labels—2,000; *presentation
folders*—5,000; *notepads*—100
Special Techniques: Double hit of Pantone 382 green on
back; die cut on business card and folder

Before creating an identity for ForSomeoneSpe-
cial.com, an online gift service, Karacters Design
Group knew their goals were to convey emotional
excitement, distinguish the service from the competition, and portray the company as sophisticated and professional before its investors.

To achieve their objective, designers focused
on the act of giving as an emotional expression of
a special relationship. "ForSomeoneSpecial.com
empowers the celebratory act of gift-giving
itself—the active interaction between gift-giver
and recipient, out of which comes the gift itself.

The three-color gift box suggests the variety and
excitement of gifts available, while the styling of
the bouncy bow at the top joins the hands of
friendship," says Nancy Wu, co-art director.

Tying it all together is a lively color palette,
which is unique amongst the competition,
according to designers. "We allowed color to play
a dominant role, balanced with the clean white-
ness of the sheet. The identity appeals to modern
shoppers and corporations," adds Wu.

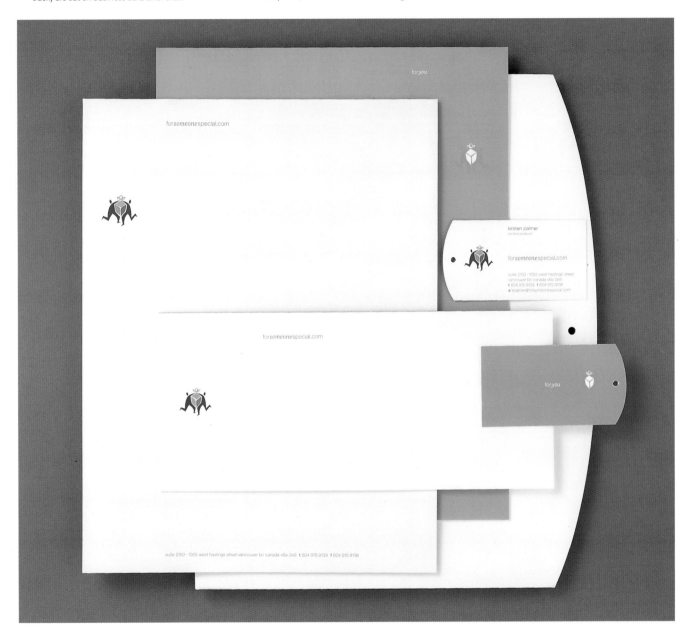

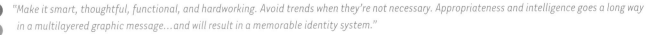

*"Make it smart, thoughtful, functional, and hardworking. Avoid trends when they're not necessary. Appropriateness and intelligence goes a long way
in a multilayered graphic message…and will result in a memorable identity system."*

NANCY WU

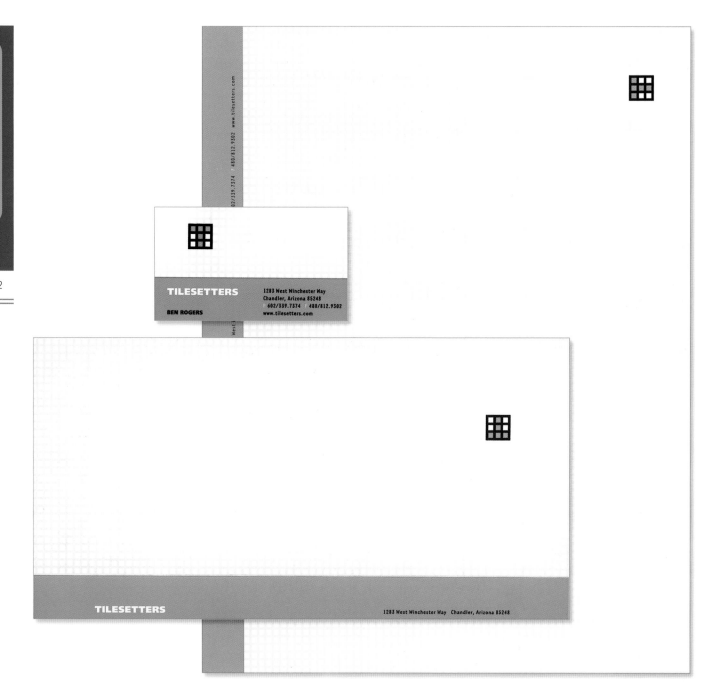

● TIP

Use the same size logo on all pieces to
save debossing die costs.

"Just because a client approaches you
with a small budget doesn't mean that
you're limited in your creativity."

SPENCER WALTERS

Tilesetters Identity

Studio: SDZYNE
Art Director/Designer: Spencer Walters
Client: Tilesetters
Paper: Via Smooth, Pure White
Colors: three match colors
Print Run: 2,000
Cost Per Unit: $1.40
Special Techniques: Custom ink for background grid

Designer Spencer Walters explains that this design
was quite straightforward. Because the client sets
tile, a debossed grid pattern was a natural choice
for the identity. "Since the client mostly uses
squares and grids, the challenge was to create
something that was creative and memorable,"
says Walters. "The use of a non-typical, bright
yellow-orange color helped achieve these goals,"
he says. He chose to deboss the logo so it appears
to be actually set into the business card, letterhead and envelope.

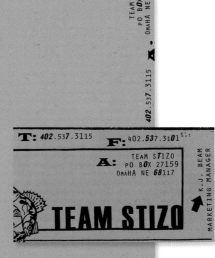

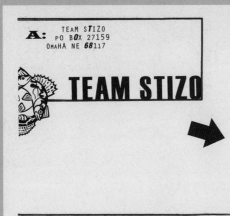

Team Stizo Identity

Studio: Archrival, Inc.
Art Director/Designer: Clint! Runge
Client: Team Stizo
Paper: French
Colors: one match color
Print Run: 500

Team Stizo, a professional fishing team that travels the pro fishing circuits, needed an identity that was simple but rough. "They remarked, 'We're looking for something we can get fingerprints and fish guts on,'" recalls Clint! Runge, art director.

Cost was a major factor in creating the system since the client had allocated most of its money for brochures. To stretch the budget, Runge used as many samples and free papers from his printer's sample room that he could get his hands on. Consequently, business cards and letterhead are printed on a variety of different papers and weights. "This helped us to achieve the feeling of a tackle box—chaotic but organized to the fisherman," says Runge.

"An identity system works when it makes the target market understand the brand. In this case, the rough, gruff nature of these fishermen contrasted with professionally designed cards and communicated that they are regular fishermen who are good at what they do."

CLINT! RUNGE

Beast of the East Identity

Studio: Sommese Design
Art Directors: Lanny Sommese, Kristin Sommese
Designer: Kristin Sommese
Illustrator: Lanny Sommese
Client: BeastOfTheEast.net
Paper: Gilbert
Colors: three match colors
Print Run: 500
Cost Per Unit: $.50 average for all
Special Techniques: Pre-existing die-cut circle on the
    envelope allows the beast's face on the letter-
    head to show through.

The BeastOfTheEast.net, a web portal, needed a
logo that appealed to a college-age audience.

Moreover, the beast image needed to be gender
neutral and irreverent—running in the face of
convention for Gen X types.

"The challenge was to create a look that
appealed to the audience. [This] was solved with
a serial image where the beast sticks its tongue
out," says Lanny Sommese, art director and illustrator. The envelope has a circular die cut where
the letterhead's Beast of the East logo can peek
out, and the accordion fold of the business card
creates a pop-up effect.

"It works because it solves the client's problem by creating an image that sets the appropriate visual tone for the company and transmits it
consistently through the call-card stationery system," says Sommese.

*"Every problem has something unique that
a creative designer can hang his or her
hat on. Find it and then let it drive your
visual approach. The more specific a
project is, the easier it is to sell."*

LANNY SOMMESE

Leapfrog Identity

Studio: Leapfrog Marketing
Art Directors: Rob Pawlik, Usa Fields,
    Dough Ghering, Jim Albright
Illustrator: Scott Sturdy
Client: Leapfrog Marketing
Paper: stationery—Neenah Classic
    Crest; *invitation*—McCoy Silk Cover
Colors: four-color process plus five
    match colors
Print Run: stationery—5,000; *invitation*—2,500
Special Techniques: Converted coin-
    style envelopes

What was the challenge in creating this identity? Finding a way for four designers and one illustrator to overcome their "frog" mentality. Designers wanted an icon that captured the company's name—Leapfrog Marketing—but they didn't want something that was too comical or too literal.

Finally, the answer came in a simple napkin sketch. "It is a very eclectic icon," says Rob Pawlik, one of several designers working on the project. "We used several individual parts and colors to form a timeless frog propelling itself forward."

This identity represents the way the team works, according to Pawlik. He explains, "It has to say 'brand' before it says your name."

TIP

Simple is better. Adding more stuff to a design is just that: more stuff.

FIND INNOVATIVE ②
answers

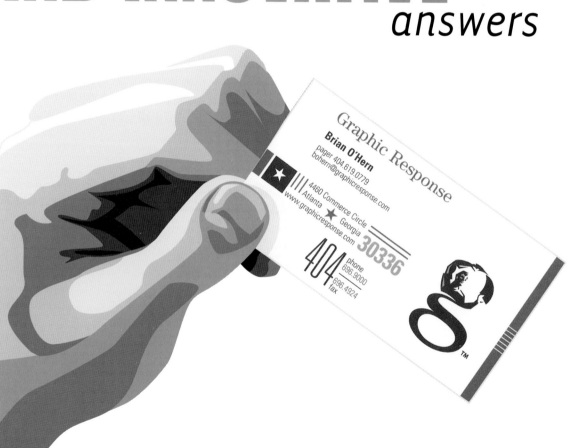

Graphic Response

Brian O'Hern
pager 404.619.0779
bohern@graphicresponse.com

4460 Commerce Circle
Atlanta ★ Georgia **30336**
www.graphicresponse.com

404 phone 696.9000
696.4924 fax

COMPUTERCAFE
ANIMATION AND VISUAL EFFECTS

715 BROADWAY SUITE 310,
SANTA MONICA, CA 90401
T. 310.395.9013 F 310.395.9814

1436 U STREET NW, SUITE 100, WASH...
WWW.KITCHENK.ORG PH 202.232.2675 FX 202.38...

GIVE YOUR CREATIVITY A JOLT AND THROW CAUTION TO THE WIND. > > > > > >

In an ideal world, an identity conveys the personality and philosophy of a company and the business it does— as well as provide
pertinent contact information. Can an identity do all these
things and be innovative, too? Too often it seems the message is
lost in a jumble of concepts, images, words, and symbols that
confuse the central message rather than enhancing it.

   The most successful identities speak with one voice. Their
messages are distilled and clear, and the design is not confused
or confusing. The designs on the following pages prove that
innovative designs are possible in every industry. Creativity need
not be at odds with strategic objectives. Not only can these two
coexist, they also can complement each other beautifully.

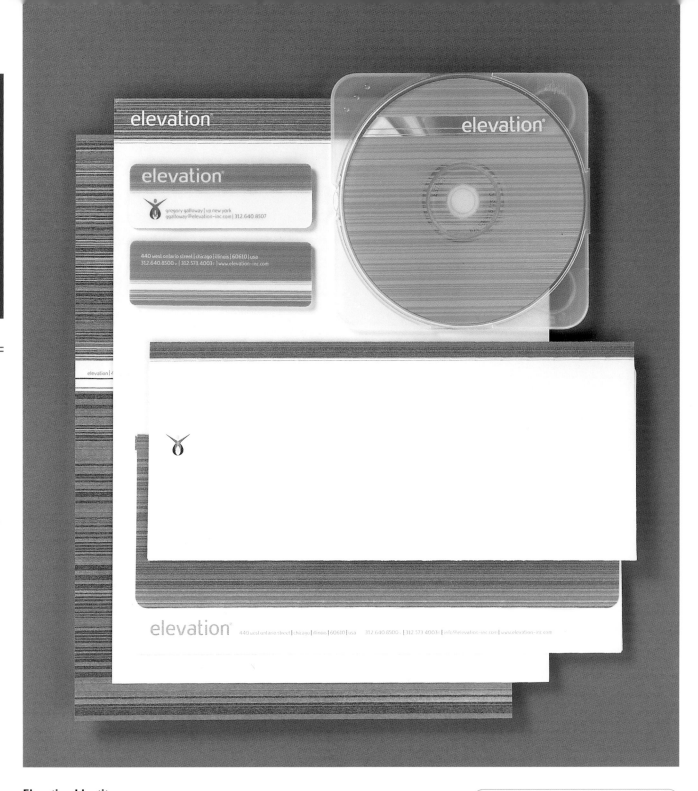

Elevation Identity

Studio: Segura, Inc.
Art Director/Designer: Carlos Segura
Client: Elevation
Colors: four match colors
Print Run: 10,000

This identity is immediately recognizable thanks to the multiple lines running through it. These lines represent the travel of information, which is the perfect visual metaphor for a company that spe-

cializes in the Internet. For designers, working with companies involved in the Internet can be tricky business. It isn't easy to "create a brand that is both modern yet classic, and one which represents technology," says Carlos Segura. Nevertheless, Segura has pulled off the challenge here.

Orage Identity

Studio: Époxy Communication, Inc.
Creative Directors: Daniel Fortin,
George Fok
Art Directors/Designers: Marc Serre,
Stéphanie Cliche

Orage, a Canadian clothing company
for skiers, received a commercial
look with a "hard edge" from
designers. They decided to include a
sled shape in the logo and colored
the identity in a cool blue palette.

TIP

*Explore the effects of
reversing a logo on different parts of the letterhead
system. Different sizes
combined with different
colors add to the versatility
of the system.*

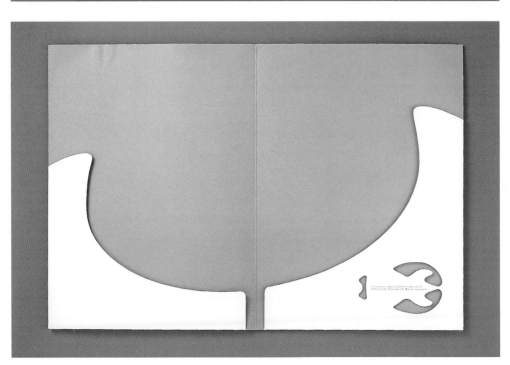

Greatlodge.com Identity

Studio: Cahan & Associates
Art Director: Bill Cahan
Client: Greatlodge.com

Greatlodge.com is an online hunting and fishing community resource. Its identity was created with vintage styling and a rich palette. The burgundy, green and gold make it evocative of the old West. The choices of type and illustration also contribute to this feeling.

TIP

When trying to evoke the past, research colors and fonts popular at the time to avoid an embarrassing mistake. For instance, manufactured hot pink colors weren't invented until the 1930s and manufactured lime green didn't come into being until the 1950s.

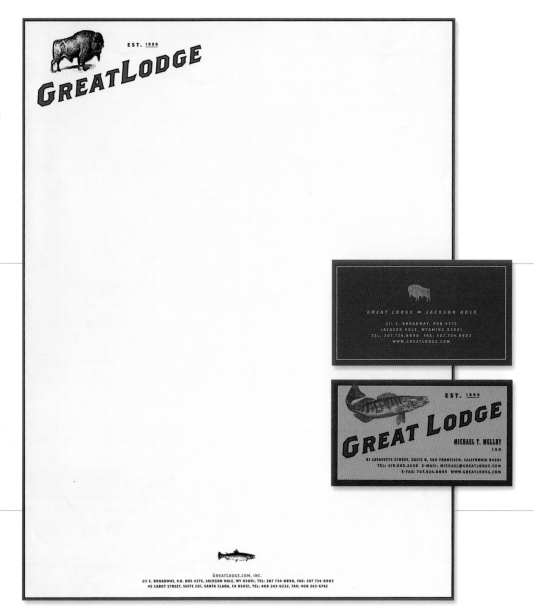

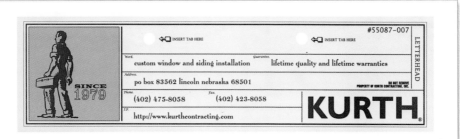

Kurth Identity

Studio: Archrival, Inc.
Art Director/Designer: Clint! Runge
Client: Kurth Contracting
Colors: two match colors
Print Run: 2,000

While most construction contractors opt for a boring one-color business card and call it a day, Kurth Contracting wanted something different. "Kurth wanted the system to be a mix of construction, aesthetics, and the trusting honest approach the family-run business gives to its clients," says

Clint! Runge, art director/designer. "The type needed to show strength at some times and at other times, needed to be detail-oriented," adds Runge.

He further explains, "There were some difficulties where we weren't sure where the system might go. In the end, the relationship made us more critical of the importance of each graphic and them more aware of how to run their brand."

"I used to think that I needed a really crazy client in order to do good work. Kurth is a great example of a 'boring' client, but one that is really interesting in their industry. Don't assume that because you find the service or client to be uninteresting that they can't carry a great design."

CLINT! RUNGE

SAFECO Ascent Identity

Studio: NBBJ Graphic Design
Art Director: Leo Raymundo
Designers: Yachun Peng, Leo Raymundo
Client: SAFECO
Paper: Mohawk Navajo
Colors: seven colors, both match and
   process
Print Run: 10,000

The challenge in creating this identity for SAFECO, an insurance company, was developing a concept that worked with the existing logo yet could stand on its own as part of a persuasive travel incentive campaign.

Inspiration came from the Canadian Rockies, mountain climbing and teamwork, which all complement SAFECO's brand attributes. Postage-stamp stickers with the word "Ascent," encourage the target audience to rise to the challenge. Likewise, the mountainscapes communicate that SAFECO always rises to a challenge.

Kelly Coller, spokesperson for NBBJ Graphic Design, says of the system, "It solves business goals, does a great job of corporate storytelling for a conservative client and entices the target audience—top insurance brokers."

TIP

Bending the rules of design is just one way of pushing back on what the eye has become accustomed to seeing. Knowing the limits of usage for an identity and being able to design around those limits to accommodate the client's needs makes an uncommon design very functional.

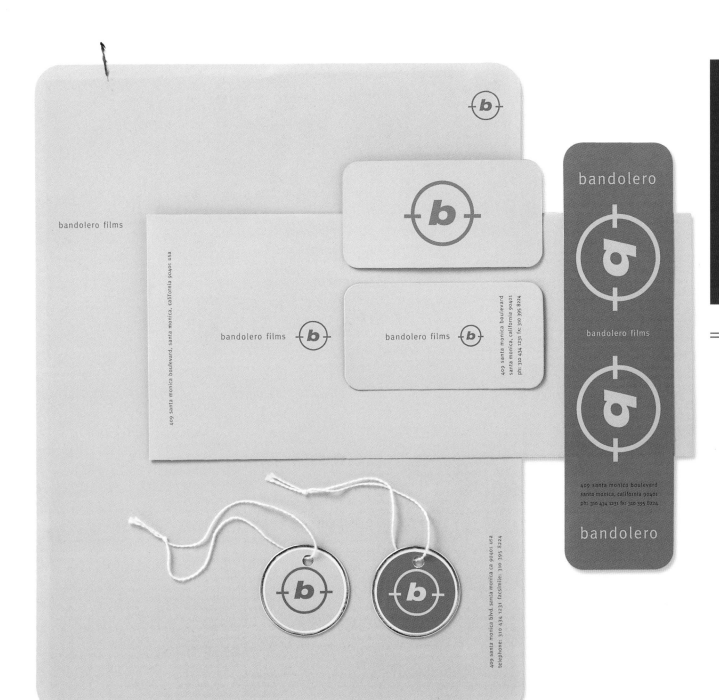

Bandolero Films Identity

Studio: Blok Design
Art Director: Vanessa Eckstein
Designers: Vanessa Eckstein, Frances Chen
Client: Bandolero Films
Paper: Carnival
Colors: three match colors
Print Run: 3,000

Bandolero is a film production company that works both in the American and Hispanic markets. The icon, developed by Blok Design, employs a "target," which hones in on the company's ability to exist across borders. "We thought it would be interesting to express this continuous flux both in the movement of color and type—keeping in mind that, as usual, we had to be cost-effective," says Vanessa Eckstein, art director.

TIP

Clue into a client's style by observing their color preferences, the company's offices and general working atmosphere. Branding must visually capture a host of intangibles: the history and protected future of a company, products and services, customer service, and mission.

TNN Stationery System

Studio: AdamsMorioka
Art Director: Noreen Morioka
Designer: Volker Dülle
Client: The National Network (TNN)
Paper: Strathmore Writing Ultimate
White Wove, 24 lb.
Colors: four match colors
Print Run: 10,000

Inspiration for this multicolored identity came from a hodgepodge of sources, including the architecture of Jean Novel, the film Airport '75, and the previous TNN logo, according to Sean Adams.

The difficult part of this job was trying to incorporate elements of the existing logo while repositioning the network as it changed from The Nashville Network to The National Network. "Using a vibrant palette and unexpected composition reinforced these ideas," says Sean Adams.

TIP

Listen to what your client tells you—and what they're really telling you. Make sure that you don't leave out any steps in the design process, particularly the design brief. Every project must be adequately researched and prepared for—and all the critical questions answered—in order for you to be equipped with all the tools you need to successfully maximize your creativity and produce exciting, effective work.

7075 Campus Rd. Moorpar

7075 Campus Rd. Moorpark, CA 93021 • 805.378.1405 • MCInstitutes@vcccd.net

TLCI Identity

Studio: Barbara Brown Marketing & Design
Art Director: Barbara Brown
Designers: Barbara Brown (logo), Jon A. Leslie (stationery)
Client: The Learning Community Institutes

The Learning Communities Institutes are geared toward high school and early-year college students interested in continuing education. "We wanted to create branding that teenagers would think was 'cool' but at the same time acknowledge that higher education is a serious matter," says Barbara Brown.

"We wanted the branding to speak directly to teenagers 15 to 18 years old, which studies show are the most wired generation yet," says Brown. The solution was found in developing a logo using USB plugs outlining three faces, which depict the process of learning: listening, processing, and that "aha!" moment. "Angled boxes create a Calder-like effect and infuse a splash of playful color," Brown adds.

"Often, branding is a customer's first connection to a company. It's essential that the logo, colors and graphics immediately show what the company stands for and what it can do for clients."

BARBARA BROWN

7075 Campus Rd. Moorpark, CA 93021 • 805.378.1405 • MCInstitutes@vcccd.net

Pearl Store Identity

Studio: [i]e design, Los Angeles
Art Director: Marcie Carson
Designer: Cya Nelson
Client: Pearl Store
Paper: Curious Iridescent Cyber Grey and Morphing Mauve, 80 lb.
Colors: three match colors
Special Techniques: Embossed business card, custom die cut on business card and envelope

Pearl, a boutique specializing in vintage couture, needed an identity that communicated a combination of rock n' roll, retro and girliness while preserving a vintage 'sea theme' in keeping with the name of the store. The task was seemingly all-encompassing, so designers needed to focus.

"We brainstormed these themes and decided on an eclectic mixture of type forms. The client, Jennifer Nicholson, uses a variety of materials, textures, and patterns in her work, including lace, feathers, chartreuse lining, chiffon, polka dots, petticoat and seersucker. These materials inspired our shapes, form, and color," says Alli Q. Neiman, [i]e design, Los Angeles.

The result is a beautifully nostalgic yet off-center identity system that appears as tactile as the fabrics it mimics.

> "We differentiate ourselves from others by admitting that our job is not to make a piece of paper look pretty. Our job is to solve problems—to place imagery and words on paper in an effort to successfully communicate what our clients need to say."
>
> ALLI Q. NEIMAN

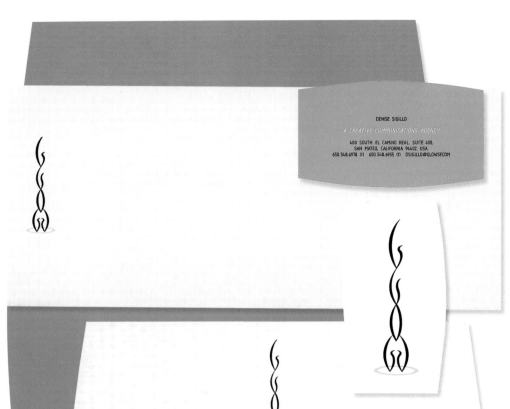

A CREATIVE COMMUNICATIONS AGENCY.

DENISE SIGILLO

A CREATIVE COMMUNICATIONS AGENCY

400 SOUTH EL CAMINO REAL, SUITE 400,
SAN MATEO, CALIFORNIA 94402, USA.
650.548.6978 (t)   650.548.6955 (f)   DSIGILLO@GLOWSF.COM

400 SOUTH EL CAMINO REAL, SUITE 400, SAN MATEO, CALIFORNIA 94402, USA. 650.548.6950 (t)   650.548.6955 (f)   WWW.GLOWSF.COM

Glow Identity

Studio: Segura, Inc.
Art Director/Designer: Carlos Segura
Client: Glow
Colors: three match colors
Special Technique: Each item has a
    custom die-cut

Glow, A Creative Communications
Agency, is a company that specializes in the Internet. They wanted to
change their name simply to Glow,
requiring a complete reinvention of
the identity. Consequently, Carlos
Segura chose to incorporate typography that reflected the glow of a
flame's energy and make the type
treatment the brand identity. Blue
was chosen as the primary focal
point of the color palette because
blue is the hottest part of a flame.
    Did it work? Yes, says Carlos
Segura, "It is elegant and graceful."

● TIP

● *Let the essence of the com-*
● *pany inspire your design.*

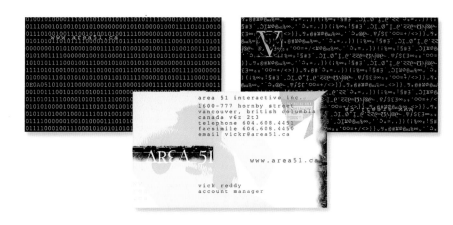

Area 51 Business Card

Studio: Karacters Design Group
Art Director/Designer: Matthew Clark
Creative Director: Maria Kennedy
Client: Area 51 Interactive
Paper: Neenah Classic Crest, Luna
Colors: three-over-three match colors

This card is cryptic and intriguing, everything that designers hoped it would be. Matthew Clark, designer, says, "If everything on the Internet is virtual, not of the tangible world, then the entire identity should follow suit." As a result, nothing was scanned in from the 'real world' in the design of this card; everything was sampled and reworked online.

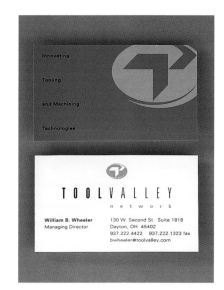

Tool Valley Network Business Card

Studio: Real Art Design Group, Inc.
Art Director: Chris Wire
Designer: Al Hidalgo
Client: Tool Valley Network
Paper: Currency
Colors: two match colors

For this regional initiative that promotes the tool and die industry, designers were inspired by metals, tools and die punches. They chose a metallic color for the palette and kept the mark clean and simple to represent the industry's move from handwork to the use of computers.

One Skinny Cook Business Card

Studio: Lloyds Graphic Design and Communication
Art Director/Designer: Alexander Lloyd
Client: One Skinny Cook
Paper: Classic Brightwater Artesian White
Colors: two match colors

The client, Jason Dell, came up with the name for his business based on his naturally lean build. That provided the inspiration for this business card's icon, which works just as well small scale as it does on the restaurant's signage.

Elements in Design Business Card

Studio: BBK Studio
Art Director/Designer: Sharon Oleniczak
Client: Mandira Gazal
Paper: Monadnock Astrolite
Colors: two match colors
Size: 2" x 2$^{1}/_{2}$"
Print Run: 1,000

Elements in Design is a Feng Shui consultation and holographic repatterning firm. With nature being so integral to the principles of Feng Shui, it was important that it be equally integral to the design of this card. Designers specified that the corners of the card be die cut to soften its edges, then modified the basic stand-alone card to work as a politically correct matchbook, which doesn't hold matches but a miniature notepad.

Owen Roberts Group Business Card

Studio: Monster Design
Art Directors/Designers: Hannah Wygal, Theresa Veranth
Client: Owen Roberts Group
Paper: Mohawk Superfine
Colors: two match colors

Embossing was added to this business card for extra dimension and texture and to draw attention to the signature logo. Interestingly, while most embosses are lost on the reverse of the paper stock, this one stands out as it is emphasized with color, a touch that adds a playful, one-last-shot impression for the recipient.

Homefield Heroes Business Card

Studio: 4th Revolution
Art Director: Tracy Roberts
Designer: Trevor Ferruggia
Paper: Neenah Classic Crest Whitestone 130 lb. cover
Colors: two-over-one, match colors
Print Run: 10,000
Cost Per Unit: $.19

Homefield Heroes sells baseball-related artwork, so designers created this card to resemble a game ticket packed with plenty of nostalgia. They created a logo that looks like a baseball insignia using a rich color palette of dark blue and burgundy, then printed it with a letterpress.

Chapman Skateboards Business Cards

Studio: Ken Rabe, Graphic Designer
Art Directors/Designers: Ken Rabe, Gregg Giuffre
Client: Chapman Skateboards
Paper: French Construction Whitewash
Colors: two match colors
Print Run: 5,000

This skateboard manufacturer is rare in that it is a family-owned business that makes its own boards. This fact, coupled with the vintage look of the factory and warehouse, inspired designers to flash back to images of 1950s gas stations and vintage order forms. "We wanted a solution that looked like it was folded up and placed in your back pocket," says Ken Rabe, art director. "Cracks were placed throughout the solid fields of color to give it that character."

Accord Insurance Brokers Business Card

Studio: Lloyds Graphic Design and Communication
Art Director/Designer: Alexander Lloyd
Client: Accord Insurance Brokers
Paper: BJ Ball Mataura Falls
Colors: four-color process
Print Run: 1,000

This insurance company broke out from a traditionally conservative industry with this card. It features original artwork and bright, highly saturated color photography, which was shot in-house with a digital camera to minimize costs. Business cards were die cut with rounded corners and laminated to make a standout impression.

GLY Construction Identity

Studio: NBBJ Graphic Design
Art Director: Leo Raymundo
Designers: Leo Raymundo, Roddy Grant
Client: GLY Construction
Paper: Strathmore Writing
Colors: two match colors plus varnish on folder
Print Run: 500–5,000

What more fitting color palette is there for a construction company than yellow—considering yellow is the color of caution signs, heavy construction equipment and hard hats? That's what designers thought when they considered they created an identity based on yellow and black, which they implemented by using solid panels of color juxtaposed with either white or stark black-and-white photography.

"The challenge was to create an identity that would push the client image into a new era and yet appear to be timeless," says Kelly Coller of NBBJ Graphic Design. "The identity also had to last for at least ten years. One of the main ideas the designers came up with was to use the eternal shape of the circle in the design and to build an identity from there that would be simple and memorable."

Designers avoided the recipient's tendency to read the company name phonetically by separating the letters with triangular-shaped dashes.

TIP

Don't be afraid to try 'dumb' ideas or make mistakes. At least you will get the bad ideas out of your system, and you may even find the solution from a most unlikely place.

Wells Fargo Bank Cup Identity

Studio: X Design Company
Art Director: Alex Valderrama
Designers: Alex Valderrama, Jen Dahlen
Client: Wells Fargo

This identity was created for Wells Fargo's annual skiing competition. Wells Fargo, a financial institution with a long-standing tradition that dates back to America's Old West, gets treated to a trip back in time with this system that pays homage to its past. Designers decided to use this illustration,

which depicts winter snow activities in the time of the stagecoach.

The illustration is repeated on the letterhead and mailing envelopes, and again on the invitation. Interestingly, the illustration is also reproduced on a vellum envelope—not on the envelope itself, but on a sticker that serves a dual purpose as a substrate for the illustration as well as a return address label.

Die-cut snowflakes dropped into the see-through envelope as fun accent graphics continue the snowscape theme.

TIP

Clearly define and extract what the identity must accomplish. Write one sentence that describes what you want the identity to communicate.

Kelling Identity

Studio: Sayles Graphic Design
Art Director: John Sayles
Designers: John Sayles, Som Intha-langsy
Client: Kelling Management
Paper: Navajo White
Colors: three match colors
Print Run: 2,000

"By using graphics that represent speech and sounds, the viewer can almost hear what the visuals are saying in the letterhead system for Kelling Management Group, a professional speakers bureau," says Sheree Clark, Sayles Graphic Design.

"Caption bubbles on Kelling's letterhead take the limelight, appearing to jump off the paper as they proclaim 'Kelling!' along with company contact information. A collage of caption bubbles creates a layered effect on the reverse of the letterhead. The graphics are supported by equally eye-catching colors of golden yellow and bright red."

TIP

Get close with your printer and develop a good working relationship. Find out what you can do for how much. Find out if they are running certain projects for other clients that they might be able to squeeze your job onto for a nominal fee.

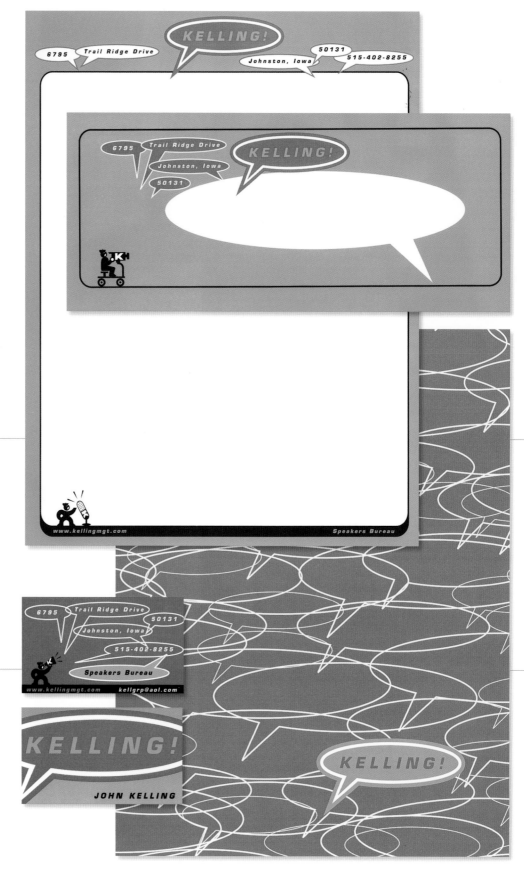

Graphic Response Identity

Studio: Jones Design Group, Inc.
Art Director: Vicky Jones
Designer: Brody Boyer
Client: Graphic Response
Paper: French Smart White
Colors: three match colors
Print Run: 4,500
Special Technique: Custom-tinted varnish run
as a dry trap

Graphic Response, a midsize offset printing company with a ten-year history, needed a new identity to keep pace with the competitive Atlanta printing market. The company was at the forefront of printing technology and needed an identity that conveyed the shop's craftsmanship and expanded services.

"The main challenge was defining what Graphic Response wanted to communicate," says Vicky Jones, art director. "After several interviews, we agreed that what differentiated Graphic Response was their pressmen's heritage, their printing experience, and the company's long history of sweeping printing award shows. The heartbeat of the company was its dedication to 'the craft of printing.'"

"The Graphic Response identity is successful because it clearly states that 'at our core, we are craftsmen, we are experts at putting ink on paper.'"

VICKY JONES

Simply She Identity

Studio: Cahan & Associates
Art Director: Bill Cahan
Designer: Sharrie Brooks
Client: Simpy She
Colors: two match colors
Print Run: 25,000

Simply She is an online source for gift cards. The identity communicates the femininity of this business by punctuating the "she" in the company name with hot pink and flood coating the backside of the business card with the same vibrant, uniquely feminine color. This is a business with a twist. If the pink hue doesn't communicate that, the tag line—which is featured on the business cards in pink, of course—certainly does: Deliciously Refreshing Communication.

 TIP

Balance creativity and flexibility with structure and guidelines; balance dynamism and current flair with classicism and longevity.

Simply She

Simply She

SimplyShe.com • Deliciously Refreshing Communication • 25 Lucerne Street, No. 1, San Francisco, CA 94103

SimplyShe.com • Deliciously Refreshing Communication • 25 Lucerne Street, No. 1, San Francisco, CA 94103 • Tel 415 522-5155 • Fax 415 522-5156

Maria Peevey
President and Founder

Deliciously Refreshing
Communication

SimplyShe.com
25 Lucerne Street, No. 1
San Francisco, CA 94103
T 415 522-5155
C 415 999-8463
F 415 522-5156
maria@simplyshe.com

Simply She

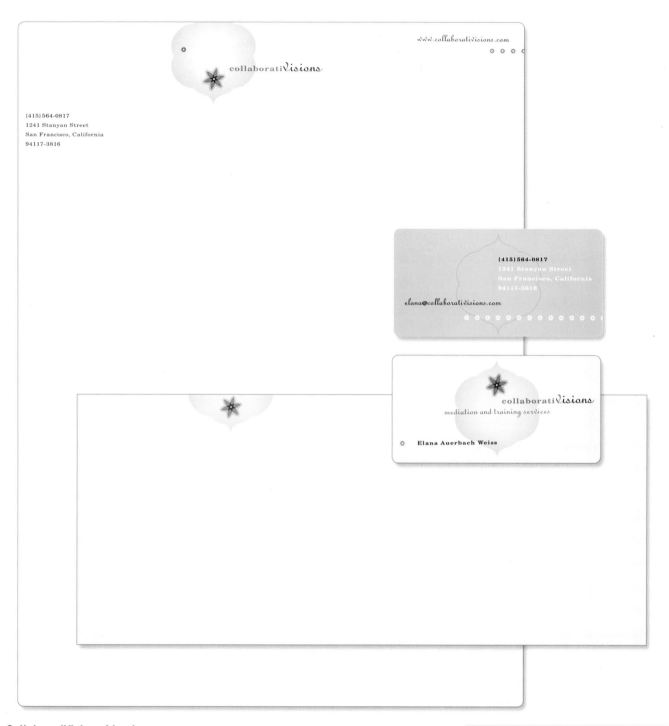

CollaboratiVisions Identity

Studio: Chen Design Associates
Art Director: Joshua C. Chen
Designer: Max Spector
Client: CollaboratiVisions
Paper: Mohawk Options True White Smooth, 130 lb. cover, 80 lb. text
Colors: two match colors
Print Run: business cards—3,000; *letterhead*—2,000
Cost Per Unit: $1.25
Special Technique: Envelope was converted to be able to print over the flap; rounded corners die cut on business cards and letterhead

"Forging new ground within the world of mediation and conflict resolution, this one-person mediation firm needed an affordable and flexible design that expressed the value of 'cultivating the peacemaker in everyone,'" says Joshua C. Chen, art director. "The inspiration and concept for the design was [taken] directly from this working philosophy and from the personality of the principal of the company."

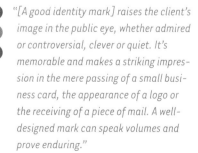

"[A good identity mark] raises the client's image in the public eye, whether admired or controversial, clever or quiet. It's memorable and makes a striking impression in the mere passing of a small business card, the appearance of a logo or the receiving of a piece of mail. A well-designed mark can speak volumes and prove enduring."

KATHRYN HOFFMAN

Watters & Watters Logo

Studio: Morris Creative, Inc.
Art Director: Steven Morris
Designer: Deanne Williamson
Client: Watters & Watters bridalwear

Frenchbread Productions Logo

Studio: Dotzero Design
Art Directors/Designers: Jon Wippich, Karen Wippich
Client: Frenchbread Productions, a recording studio
Colors: four-color process

DOGinc. Logo

Studio: Louviere & Vanessa
Art Director/Designer: Jeff Louviere
Client: DOGinc., a local nonprofit group of dog park patrons

Secret Stuff Logo

Studio: Gee + Chung Design
Art Director/Designer: Earl Gee
Client: Symantec Corporation, a company that produces encryption software
Colors: PMS 185, process black

Gladstone Logo

Studio: Parker White
Art Director: Cindy White
Designer: Dave Blank
Client: Gladstone Catering and Event Services

by Watters & Watters

Frenchbread
PRODUCTIONS

DOGinc.
DOG OWNERS GROUP, INC.

SRTECE   FTFSU
NORTON   TFSUF
SECRET   STUFF
ERSCET   FUFTS
TERECS   UFTSF

gladstone

J Records Logo

Studio: Platinum Design, Inc.
Art Director/Designer: Mike Joyce
Client: J Records/Clive Davis
(record label)
Color: PMS 2748

Fetish Kings Logo

Studio: Dotzero Design
Art Directors/Designers: Jon Wippich,
Karen Wippich
Client: Fetish Kings (jazz/rock band)

Oncalls Logo

Studio: CFX Creative
Art Director/Designer: Carly H.
Franklin
Client: Oncalls.com, a web-based
scheduling system for physicians
and hospitals

Wacky Logo

Studio: Greteman Group
Art Directors: Sonia Greteman, James
Strange
Designer: James Strange
Client: City of Wichita, KS (the logo
was used for the city's Summer of
Discovery program)

ConstructionJobs.com Logo

Studio: Parker White
Art Director: Dylan Jones
Designer: Asa Carlsson
Client: ConstructionJobs.com,
an online recruiter for the
construction industry

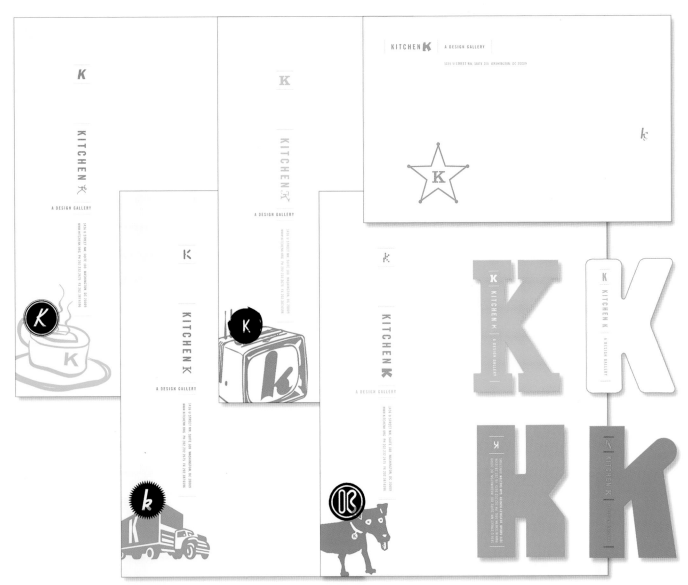

Kitchen [K] Identity Package

Studio: Kinetik, Inc.

Design Team: Jeff Fabian, Sam Shelton, Mila Arrisus-
no, Beth Clawson, Maria Fischer, Richard Fischer,
M. Jenny Harrington, Beverley Hunter, Ali Koois-
tra, Katie Kroener, Stephen Oster, Jackie Ratsch,
Scott Rier, Kamomi Solidum, Jason Thompson,
Matt Wahl

Client: Kitchen [K]—A Design Gallery, Inc.

Paper: Mohawk Navajo

Colors: four match colors

Size: All standard except for business cards which are
die cut into "K" shapes and are approximately
$2^1/_2$" x $3^3/_4$" (6 cm x 9.5 cm)

Print Run: letterhead—5,000 each of 4 versions;
envelopes—10,000; business cards—500 each of
8 versions

Cost Per Unit: letterhead—$.04; envelopes—$.18;
business cards—$.40

Special Techniques: Different dies were created for
each business "K" card; labels were printed in
one-color and the second color (black) was
printed at the same time as the address.

Kitchen [K] is a Washington, DC-based design
gallery, dedicated to all aspects of design. When
the Kinetik, Inc. design team set out to create a
new identity for the gallery, its focus was limited
to kitchen elements, but designers felt like that
solution was far too easy.

"The challenge was to come up with something that felt neutral, like a blank gallery wall,
but didn't make the gallery seem too sterile. Even
though the gallery's focus is graphic design, its
exhibition schedule includes all disciplines of
design. Therefore, the 'K' solution started to
represent the differences," says Sam Shelton,
one member of the design team.

The identity is indeed energetic. The bright
color palette pops off the printed page and view-
ers get wrapped up in all the design variations.
"It's fun and people have loved receiving the
various pieces of the letterhead. Typically a
person does not stop at one card, but rather
collects all eight of the 'K' cards," adds Shelton.

*"An identity mark should be easy for the
client to understand and use, allowing
for internal staff to embrace it to its
fullest extent."*

SAM SHELTON

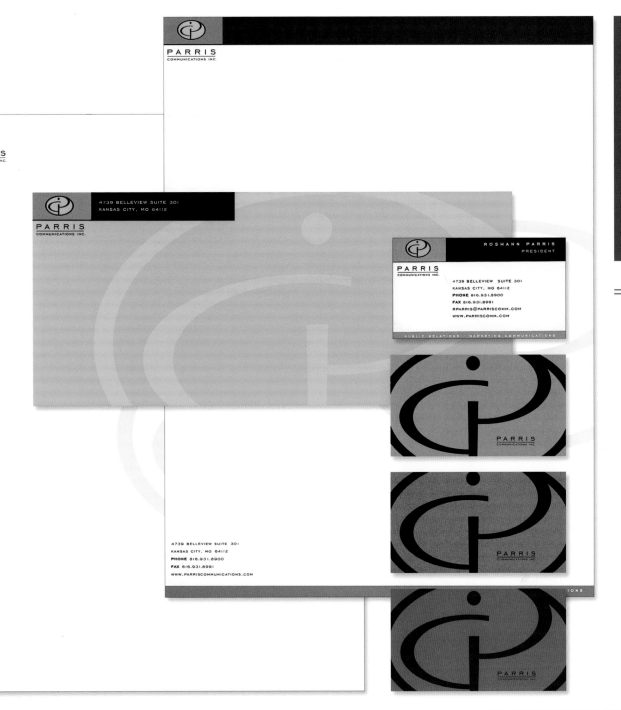

Parris Communications Identity

Studio: Willoughby Design Group
Art Director: Ann Willoughby
Designer: Derek Colling
Client: Parris Communications
Colors: four match colors

Parris Communications, a marketing/public relations firm, tapped Willoughby Design Group for its stationery, business cards and press kit. The result is a colorful system that not only complements the client's newly designed offices but offers built-in flexibility for customized communications.

TIP

Spend time up front to do competitive research. Take a look at the letterhead systems of other companies in the same industry as your client, notice television commercials, look at billboards. What are they doing and how can you do it better? This research provides you with information that's necessary to create an identity that really stands apart from the competition.

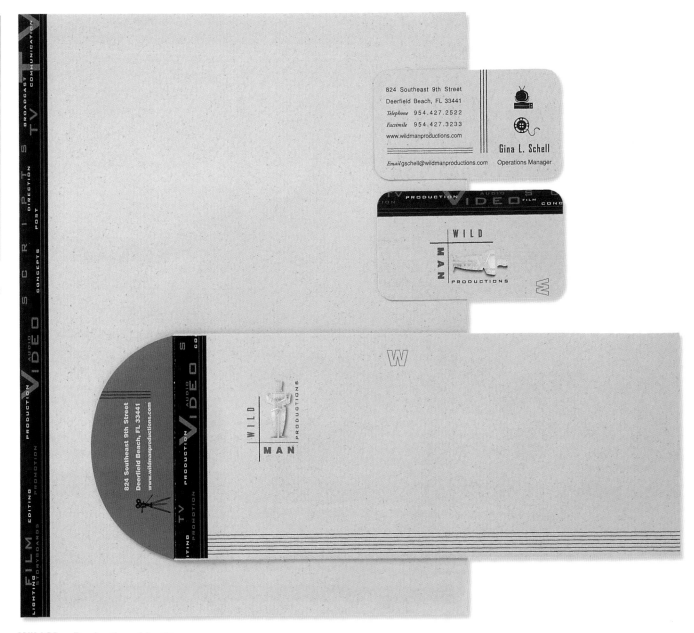

Wild Man Productions Identity

Studio: Greteman Group
Art Directors: Sonia Greteman, James Strange
Creative Director: Sonia Greteman
Designers: James Strange, Garrett Fresh
Client: Wild Man Productions
Colors: two match colors plus foil stamp
Special Technique: Special foil was used on the
  envelopes so they could be run through a
  laser printer

Wild Man Productions is a video and film production company, so the icon developed for the company by Greteman Group is especially
appropriate—the figure of a man with a filmstrip
where his head should be. "This logo celebrates
the name of the production company by using an

icon of a man restrained in a straight jacket to
play off the name," says Sonia Greteman.

Moreover, designers maximize their color
palette by printing on colored paper, which gives
the system the effect of being printed in three
colors, not just two.

*"Always try to break new ground. Don't
rely on what you've tried before. It's
better to be over the top and funky
than to be safe."*

SONIA GRETEMAN

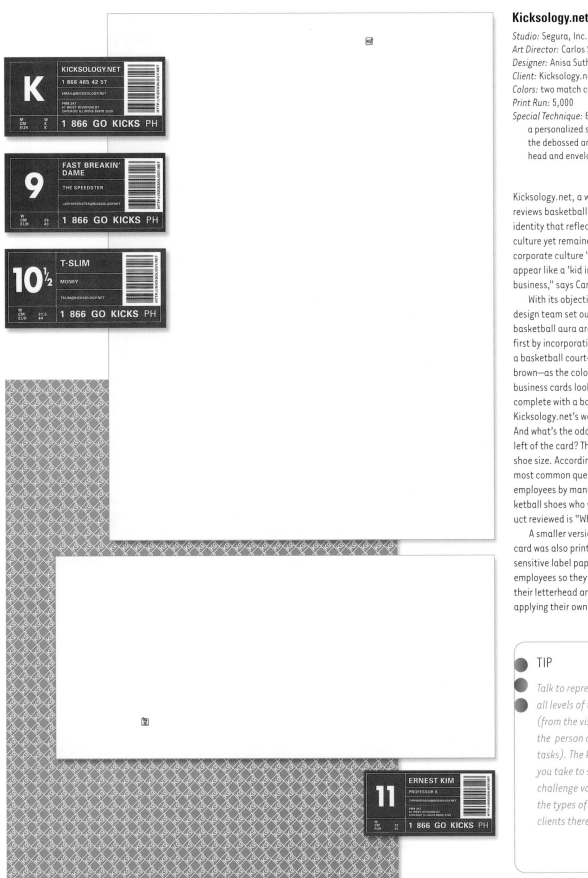

Kicksology.net Identity

Studio: Segura, Inc.
Art Director: Carlos Segura
Designer: Anisa Suthayalai
Client: Kicksology.net
Colors: two match colors
Print Run: 5,000
Special Technique: Each employee has a personalized sticker to apply to the debossed area of the letterhead and envelope

Kicksology.net, a web site that reviews basketball shoes, wanted an identity that reflected the youth culture yet remained serious to the corporate culture "so as not to appear like a 'kid in a basement' business," says Carlos Segura.

With its objectives in mind, the design team set out to create a basketball aura around this identity, first by incorporating the colors of a basketball court—orange and brown—as the color palette. The business cards look like tickets, complete with a bar code alongside Kicksology.net's web site address. And what's the odd number on the left of the card? The employee's shoe size. According to Segura, the most common question asked of employees by manufacturers of basketball shoes who want their product reviewed is "What's your size?"

A smaller version of the business card was also printed on pressure-sensitive label paper and given to employees so they can personalize their letterhead and envelopes by applying their own stickers.

TIP

Talk to representatives from all levels of the organization (from the visionary head to the person carrying out the tasks). The kind of approach you take to solve the design challenge varies as greatly as the types of industries and clients there are out there.

Claddagh Identity

Studio: Lodge Design Co.
Designer: Eric Kass
Client: Claddagh Irish Pub
Paper: French Dur-o-Tone Newsprint
Extra White, French Speckletone
Starch White, French Speckletone
Oatmeal, Chipboard
Colors: three match colors
Print Run: 1,000
Special Technique: Chipboard mailer is
letterpress printed with metallic
gold; metallic gold is used on vari-
ous uncoated paper colors to
achieve a historic yet upscale feel

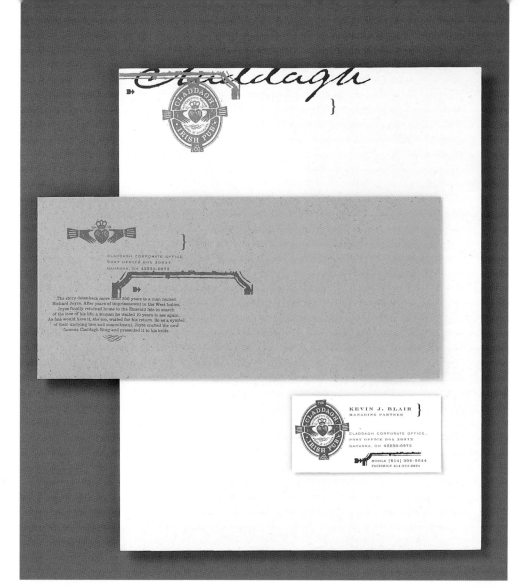

The challenge in creating the identity for this Irish pub was to express
the historical and emotional senti-
ment of the pub in its stationery
system. The Claddagh Irish Pub is a
growing chain of very authentic Irish
pubs. "Nearly every piece of furniture, fixture, antique and mural are
imported from Ireland. The identity
needed to reflect that same attention to detail and history," says Eric
Kass, designer.

Kass achieved this with a combination of warm ink and paper colors,
coupled with letterpress printing.
"The logo was inspired by antique
beer labels and was distressed to
give it an aged character. The layout
is somewhat haphazard to seem as if
it has been added to and subtracted
from over the years by different
printers. Ink colors and paper stocks
mirror the rich woods, dark beers
and warm charm found in the pub."

 TIP

*Find out what differentiates
your client. Every company is
competing with others and
needs to express its own
unique point of difference.*

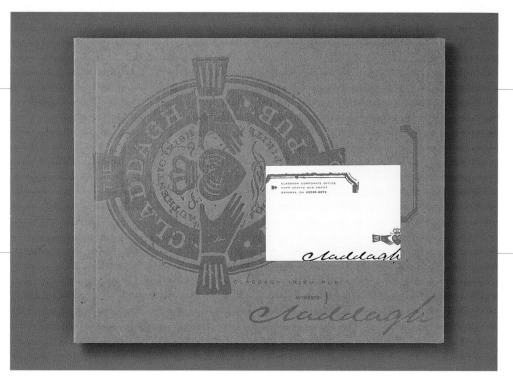

Virginia Harris Identity

Studio: Shelby Designs & Illustrates
Art Director/Designer: Shelby Putnam Tupper
Client: Virginia Harris Design, LLC
Paper: Neenah Classic Crest
Colors: two match colors
Print Run: letterhead—1000; *business card*—500;
   envelope—1500; *labels*—500
Cost Per Unit: letterhead—$.42; *business card*—$1.37;
   envelope—$.47; *A-2 notecards*—$1.08; *A-2
   envelopes*—$.48; *labels*—$.84
Special Techniques: Registered emboss on business
   card; printed both sides

"Interior design is a subjective business—dependent on converging tastes. We wanted to create a symbol that represented 'individual attention' so we gave it a hand-hewn look juxtaposed with a compelling asexual color treatment," says Shelby Putnam Tupper.

The most significant challenge, according to Tupper, was giving the client the monogram look she requested. Initially, the client wanted a very classic monogram with a "V" and an "H" or a "V," "H," and "D." Once Tupper went to work on the project, the monogram concept evolved into a very simple hand-hewn "V," which wasn't too specific. "Even in her advertising, we never use any photos—that way no one is alienated at first glance," says Tupper.

> "If the client is happy and is able to generate excitement, credibility and additional revenue from his or her audience, the identity is successful. Beauty and client appreciation are the luscious frosting on that cake."
>
> SHELBY PUTNAM TUPPER

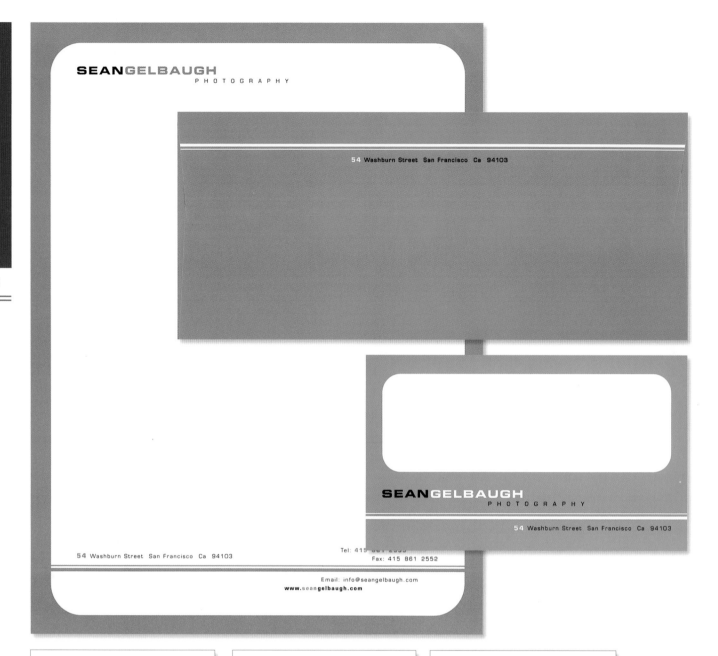

Sean Gelbaugh Identity

Studio: Super Natural Design
Art Directors: Christie Rixford, Hajdeja Ehline
Designer: Christie Rixford
Client: Sean Gelbaugh
Paper: Starwhite Tiara
Colors: three match colors plus black
Print Run: 1,000
Special Technique: Converted envelope to get a
full-color bleed

Bright green, orange and blue are the distinguishing characteristics of this photographer's identity system. Designers wanted each piece to be slightly different but to work within a system, and using different colors provided a means to stand out. Designing around the budget posed a problem, but designers easily overcame it by using lightweight paper stocks and ganging the labels in the press run.

"This identity system works because it's clean, bold and bright—just like this photographer's work."

CHRISTIE RIXFORD

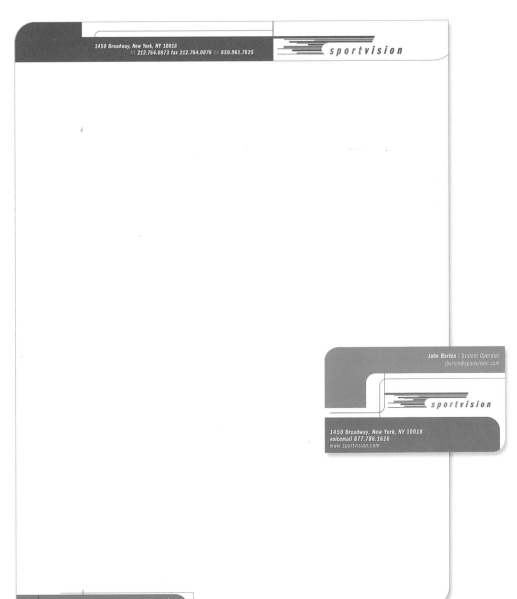

Sportvision Identity

Studio: Platinum Design, Inc.
Art Director: Vickie Peslak
Designer: Kelly Hogg
Client: Sportvision
Paper: two match colors
Print Run: 1,000
Special Technique: Die cuts

Sportvision, a start-up enterprise in need of an identity system, is a provider of technology for sports television. For inspiration for this design, designers watched lots of sports programming, then developed the color palette of blue and green on a white background to ensure longevity. The kinetic lines of the piece help portray a company that is fresh and action-oriented.

"This one just feels right. It has a natural ability to work in motion, which was an added bonus when seen on-air."

VICKIE PESLAK

Little Blue Furniture Identity

Studio: Willoughby Design Group
Art Director: Ann Willoughby
Designer: Maiko Kununishi
Client: Little Blue Furniture
Paper: Mohawk Navajo, coaster stock
Colors: two match colors
Special Techniques: Letterpress print-
ing; the use of heavy blotter paper

Subtlety is the cornerstone of this
identity system where metallic
silver and light blue work together
in harmony for a very elegant presentation. The border around the
letterhead and label system, which
is printed on blotter stock, adds a
touch of panache. Designers make
the name more memorable by color-
ing the word "blue" in the company's
name.

TIP

*Keep your eyes open! No
detail is too small and no
landscape too big to become
your inspiration.*

Digital Planet Identity

Studio: Dotzero Design
Art Directors: Karen Wippich, John Wippich, Marie Murphy, Dave Erlfrey
Designers: Karen Wippich, Jon Wippich
Client: Digital Planet
Paper: Zanders Chromolux, Cougar
Colors: business card—four-over-three match colors; *letterhead*—three-over-two; *folder*—one-over-six; *envelope*—four-color process
Print Run: folders—5,000; *letterhead*—10,000; *business cards*—36 different names
Special Techniques: Folders coated silver on one side and embossed; business cards have a variety of backs (some employees picked which backs they wanted)

This multifaceted identity has plenty of aspects worth discussing. Designers point out that the logo itself is not only a planet, but also a tilted *d* and a tilted *p*. The bolt of electricity signifies electronic online broadcasting—the client's niche. The identity looks like it came out of a total creative free fall, but designers had to be careful not to go too far. "It needed to appeal to a young audience, but also to potential investors," says Jon Wippich. "The bright, colorful illustrations give it a fun feel while the information sides are more straightforward and orderly."

TIP

Push beyond the ordinary: Don't simply stick the logo and copy anywhere on the page. A good logo will get noticed, but the way in which it fits into the whole identity package determines how effective it will be.

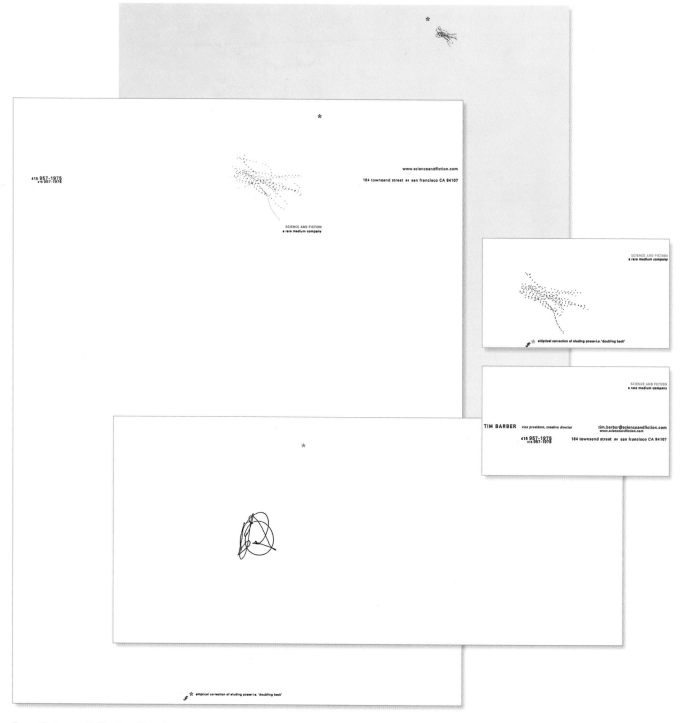

Rare Science & Fiction Identity

Studio: Cahan & Associates
Art Director: Bill Cahan
Designer: Jean Orlebeke
Client: Rare Science & Fiction
Paper: Mohawk Superfine Ultrawhite Eggshell
Colors: three-color letterpress plus one color litho
Print Run: 5,000

"The company's name is a metaphor for what they do," says Jean Orlebeke, designer on the project.

"'Science & Fiction' represents technology and entertainment in the world of interactive media design. To convey this, we chose scientific diagrams that represented forms of entertainment and historical events. We chose letterpressing to give the pieces weight and texture and to add a new design element to a company that never gets to use paper."

TIP

Don't mangle or force type into unnatural positions. Pay your dues. Absorb. Learn. Work hard and late. Always remember— this is commercial art, not fine art.

THE **BLUE ROCK**

EDITING COMPANY

▪ 575 ▪ LEXINGTON ▪ AVENUE ▪ NEW YORK ▪ NY ▪ 10022 ▪ USA ▪ 212 ▪ 752 ▪ 3348 ▪ t ▪ 212 ▪ 752 ▪ 0307 ▪ f ▪ INFO@BLUEROCKNY.COM ▪

THE **BLUE ROCK**

EDITING COMPANY

▪ DAVID ▪ CORNMAN ▪
▪ EDITOR ▪

BR

THE **BLUE ROCK**

EDITING COMPANY

▪ 575 ▪ LEXINGTON ▪ AVENUE ▪ NEW YORK ▪ NY ▪ 10022 ▪ USA ▪
▪ 212 ▪ 752 ▪ 3348 ▪ t ▪ 212 ▪ 752 ▪ 0307 ▪ f ▪
▪ INFO@BLUEROCKNY.COM ▪

The Blue Rock Identity

Studio: Segura, Inc.
Art Director/Designer: Carlos Segura
Client: The Blue Rock Editing Company
Colors: four-color process
Print Run: 10,000

In developing this identity, Carlos Segura sought inspiration from the company's name—The Blue Rock Editing Company—and based the concept on that. The toughest part was finding a look that could be adapted to a number of applications required by the client. Segura knew the system was successful when it made the client happy.

TIP

Take the time to develop your talent and business sense so you can keep and inspire clients. The greatest designer in the world may never be recognized if he or she has a shoddy business practice because he or she will never be able to keep a job or clients.

radian

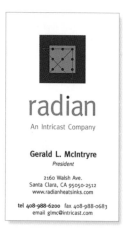

radian

An Intricast Company

Gerald L. McIntryre
President

2160 Walsh Ave.
Santa Clara, CA 95050-2512
www.radianheatsinks.com

tel 408-988-6200 fax 408-988-0683
email glmc@intricast.com

Thermal Leaders By Design

2160 Walsh Ave.
Santa Clara, CA 95050-2512

tel 408-988-6200
fax 408-988-0683
www.radianheatsinks.com

Radian Identity

Studio: Wallop Design Group
Art Director: Patrik Kusek
Designer: Nicole Sorensen
Client: Radian Heatsinks
Colors: two match colors

"Inspiration for the logo was based on 'thinking outside the box' and the unique problem solving capabilities of the client who specializes in heat sinks," says Patrik Kusek about Radian's identity, which literally uses a box and places a pattern outside of its borders. "The logo illustrates the unique selling proposition of creative problem solving from heat sink design to manufacturing."

● TIP

Any good design is a solution to a visual problem, so it must have a strong concept. However, concept alone won't complete the picture. You have to be able to make it look good, too. How does one accomplish that? Well, short of having pure raw talent, a firm grasp of the design aesthetic helps tremendously. Read design magazines, know design history and seek out design heroes.

Mimmo Design Business Card

Studio: Mimmo Design
Designer: Kevin L. Robinson
Colors: four-color digital print

This business card was created using four-color digital output, which is printed as needed in-house. Two tiny die cuts add distinction and the series of four different color schemes further the visual interest. "It is always difficult to create an identity system to set yourself apart from others," says Kevin L. Robinson, designer. "You just keep trying until you think you've got it."

Milieu Interior Design

Studio: Digital Slant
Art Director: Cami Boehme
Designer: Steven Schaelling
Client: Milieu Design
Paper: Neenah Classic Laid
Colors: three match colors
Size: 2" x 6$^{1}/_{2}$" (5 cm x 17 cm)
Print Run: 1,000
Special Technique: Die-cut on business cards

Milieu Design, an interior design firm, needed an identity that reflected the diversity of its work, which ranges from interiors and landscaping to furniture design and community planning. To that end, designers created a logo that's flexible enough to encompass all four areas, then chose natural colors and textured papers to tie all four disciplines together. The card works like a matchbook with a die cut that the logo slips into.

Ergonet Business Card

Studio: Époxy Communication, Inc.
Creative Directors: Daniel Fortin, George Fok
Art Directors/Designers: George Fok, Stéphanie Cliché

The logo on this business card, an arrow, represents direction, interactivity, technology and the future. The letter "Ɛ" stands for the client's name, Ergonet, and also for e-commerce.

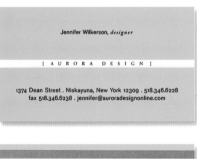

Aurora Design Business Cards

Studio: Aurora Design
Designer: Jennifer Wilkerson
Paper: Mohawk Superfine Ultrawhite Smooth 130 lb.
Colors: four-color process plus match yellow and overall aqueous coating
Print Run: 1,000 each of 6
Cost Per Unit: $.04

As Jennifer Wilkerson reviewed her portfolio, she realized how important color is to her from both a professional and personal standpoint. With that in mind, she knew she had to integrate color into her identity. As a result, she has a rainbow-inspired card that is vibrant and eye-catching and also reflects the nature of her work.

Metro Electric Identity

Studio: Archrival, Inc.
Art Director/Designer: Allen Boe
Client: Metro Electric Company of
Omaha
Colors: three match colors

This simple letterhead system presents an interesting problem. Metro Electric Company of Omaha is licensed in six different states and bids on jobs in each state. Designers needed to address this issue by creating an element that would communicate the company's ability to do business in multiple states. "The solution was to list the states with corresponding circles," explains Allen Boe, designer. "Then, Metro could knock out what state the letter or bid was being sent to."

A series of graphics and icons that represent electrical functions, along with hot and cool colors to represent positive and negative charges, dress up the system.

*"An identity should visually
speak the language of
the company to the
audience."*

ALLEN BOE

WebAppFactory Identity

Studio: Chen Design Associates
Art Director: Joshua C. Chen
Designer: Max Spector
Client: WebAppFactory, Inc.
Paper: envelopes—French Dur-o-Tone
 Brown Packaging Wrap, 70 lb. text;
 media kit, business cards—French
 Speckletone Chocolate Vellum 100
 lb. cover; *letterhead*—Neenah
 Classic Crest; *labels*—MACtac
 StarLiner Blinding White
Colors: three match colors
Print Run: letterhead—5,000; *media
 folders, envelopes*—1,000;
 assorted labels—2,400–3,600;
 metal business cards—150
Cost Per Unit: $6.50
Special Techniques: Acid etching; laser
 cutting; foil stamping; debossing;
 hole-punching; and hand-applied
 labeling

WebAppFactory, Inc. is a web
applications development company
that likes the combination of the old
economy with its industrial connota-
tions and the new economy with its
high-tech overtones. Consequently,
the designer's challenge was to
combine the two elements visually.

"The *Factory* in WebAppFactory
speaks to the work ethic and 'can do'
attitude of the company's employees,
as well as suggesting permanence,
dependability and strength. The
trademark employs a series of holes,
which fit onto a very simple, modular
grid to make up the letterforms—WAF.
The holes themselves symbolize rivets,
holes from a punch card or electronic
circuitry," says Joshua Chen, art
director.

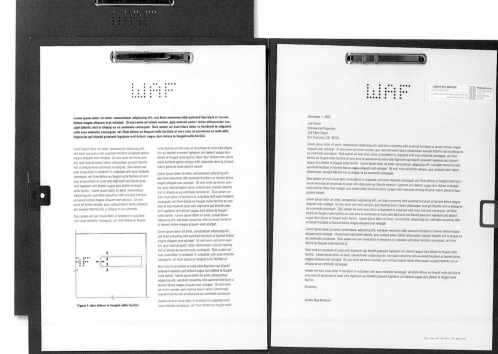

TIP

Break some rules!

Q Quant Logo

Studio: Platinum Design, Inc.
Art Director: Vickie Peslak
Designer: Kelly Hogg, Patricia Kelleher
Client: VS Research, a market
research company

Green Tags Logo

Studio: Dotzero Design
Art Directors/Designers: Jon Wippich,
Karen Wippich
Client: Bonneville Environmental
Foundation, a nonprofit organi-
zation that promotes the use
of wind- and water-generated
power
Colors: PMS 5787, PMS 5625

Fan Pimp Logo

Studio: Olive
Art Director/Designer: Stephen Fritz
Client: Music industry software

X Nucleus Logo

Studio: X Design Company
Art Director/Designer: Alex
Valderrama
Client: X Nucleus Strategic
Branding System

iZoom Logo

Studio: Headwerk, LLC
Art Director/Designer: Erik Weber
Client: iZoom, an internet auto
racing site

Queen of Sheba Logo

Studio: Dotzero Design
Art Directors/Designers: Jon Wippich,
    Karen Wippich
Client: Queen of Sheba Ethiopian
    Restaurant
Colors: PMS 4495, PMS 130

Ghormley Construction Logo

Studio: Catapult Strategic Design
Art Director/Designer: Peter Jones
Client: Ghormley Construction

Ripe Logo

Studio: BBK Studio
Art Director: Yang Kim
Designers: Yang Kim, Kevin
    Budelmann
Client: Ripe clothing and accessories
    store

R. Messner Logo

Studio: Greteman Group
Art Director: Sonia Greteman, James
    Strange
Designer: James Strange
Client: R. Messner Construction Com-
    pany, specializing in the design
    and construction of churches

Studio Voodoo Logo

Studio: BL_NK
Art Director/Designer: Dave Blank
Client: Studio Voodoo, an after-hours
    creative social outlet

El Zanjon Identity

Studio: Blok Design
Art Director: Vanessa Eckstein
Designers: Vanessa Eckstein, Frances Chen, Stephanie Yung
Client: El Zanjon
Paper: Strathmore
Colors: four match colors
Print Run: 3,000–5,000

El Zanjon, a monument and events center, was merely a historic building in Argentina before its restoration. To coincide with its unveiling, an identity was needed that presented the new El Zanjon. "Our challenge was to make this identity as complex and as reflective of the many historical layers as the building itself," says Vanessa Eckstein.

Designers pored over examples of historical graphics and typography reflected in Buenos Aires ephemera, including tiles from the 1860s, old city maps, original illustrations and photos of the building at various states of development to create the identity.

"The design becomes a continuation of the restoration process itself," says Eckstein.

TIP

It is easy to get noticed, but to get noticed responsibly as a designer is another issue. Looking for new and unique ways to break convention and challenge industry standards is always exciting. Remember, though that everything should be done for a reason!

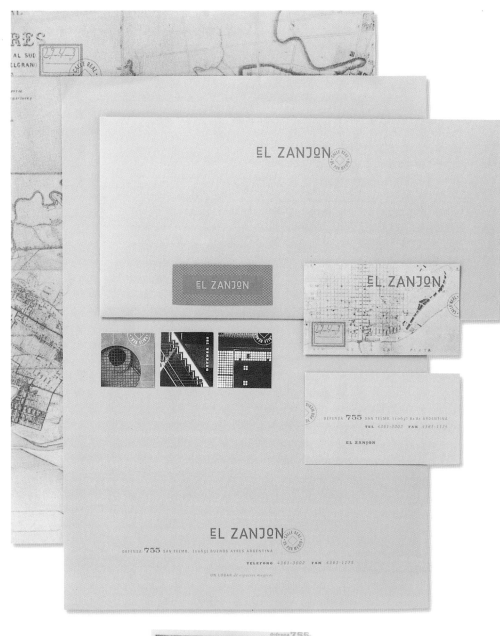

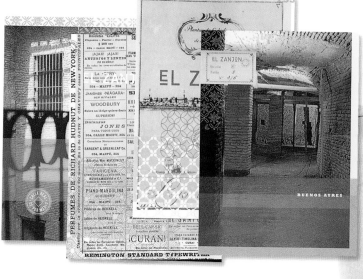

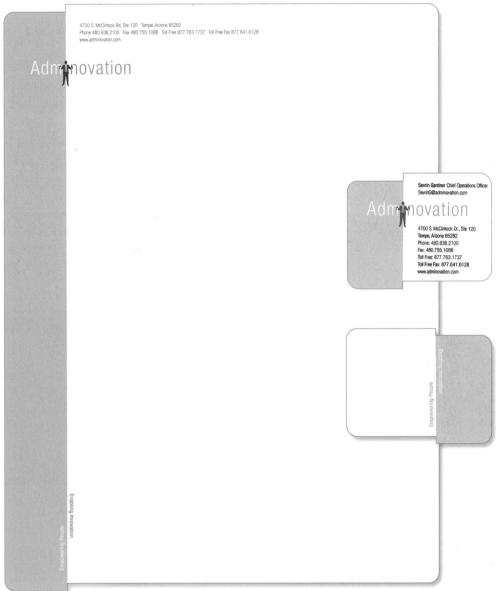

Adminovation Identity

Studio: Catapult Strategic Design
Art Director/Designer: Art Lofgreen
Client: Adminovation
Paper: ViaSmooth, Pure White, 70 lb.
Colors: three match colors
Print Run: 5,000
Cost Per Unit: $.63

Adminovation provides innovative staffing and office administration services for its clients. Designer Art Lofgreen developed this identity, which graphically portrays what the company does—it brings qualified people together with the latest technology. He broke the stationery into two parts and made it look as though the person in the logo is uniting both parts.

"It only works if it is memorable, unique, applicable to a wide array of mediums, conveys a sense of what the company does, and helps to position the company accurately."

ART LOFGREEN

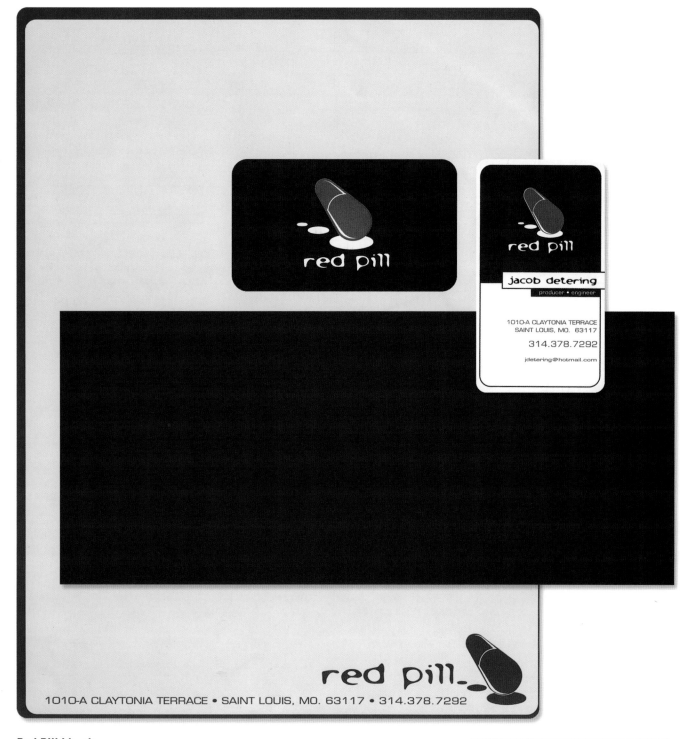

Red Pill Identity

Studio: Zn30 Creative
Art Director/Designer: Kenneth Zarecki
Client: Red Pill
Paper: Gilbert Chadwick Gray
Colors: two match colors
Print Run: 500+
Special Techniques: One-color letterhead reduced printing costs and allowed designers to fit a die cut into the budget

What was the biggest challenge with this design? "Overcoming the obvious solution of using the color red and the image of a pill," says Kenneth Zarecki, art director/designer. So why then does the identity feature red and the image of a pill?

"Oh, well, the client is always right. Right?" Zarecki says.

The imagery may not be what the designer had in mind, but the final solution works perfectly for this company, a recording studio.

 TIP

If your client doesn't want an envelope, don't try to talk them into spending $2,500 on a custom-made square-flap, translucent envelope with color bleeds.

Litho Press Business Card

Studio: Lodge Design Co.
Designer: Eric Kass
Client: Litho Press Inc.
Paper: White gloss coated
Colors: six match colors
Print Run: 5,000
Special Techniques: Die cut pops out to stand at attention; six spot colors, some of which are Day-Glo ink

This offset printer has been in business since 1953 and takes pride in its service, so it made sense to feature "a competent pressman hoisting the Litho nomenclature into the air with pride while dressed in his period printing togs," says Eric Kass, designer.

@alans Business Card

Studio: Alan Brooks Design, Inc.
Art Director/Designer: Alan Brooks
Client: @alans
Paper: Genesis Milkweed
Colors: two match colors

@alans, a computer café, appeals to a young, energetic crowd, and these words describe the personality of the café as well. To reflect his client's character, designer Alan Brooks chose vibrant green ink and used retro artwork to give the card punch. With a unique die cut creating an asymmetrically angled card, it communicates with even more panache.

Nickelodeon Business Card

Studio: AdamsMorioka
Art Director: Sean Adams
Designers: Sean Adams, Volker Dürre, Brian Hunt
Client: Nickelodeon
Colors: four match colors

"The idea that the world of Nickelodeon is bigger than the piece of paper drove this design," says Sean Adams, art director. To that end, designers redesigned the logo shapes using abstract shapes rather than iconic shapes of blimps, rocket ships, etc. Doing so allowed for a more energetic approach that speaks to children as well as advertisers and the financial community.

Urban Exposure Business Card

Studio: Sayles Graphic Design
Art Director: John Sayles
Designers: John Sayles, Som Inthalangsy
Client: Urban Exposure Mobile Advertising
Paper: Navajo White
Colors: four match colors
Print Run: 5,000

Urban Exposure Mobile Advertising's business card features a logo treatment that, when coupled with a die cut, looks like skyscrapers at different heights. Other urban icons—taxis, buses, banners and vans—appear to traffic in and out of the card.

Jennifer Nicholson Identity

Studio: [i]e design, Los Angeles
Art Director: Marcie Carson
Designers: Marcie Carson, Cya Nelson
Client: Jennifer Nicholson
Paper: Strathmore Natural White Smooth Text
Colors: Match colors
Special Techniques: Special die used for the hangtag;
    converted envelope; labels made of damask

Jennifer Nicholson, a vintage couture designer,
was opening her own store and hired [i]e design to
create her logo, letterhead and clothing labels.
The challenge: the logo had to be small enough to
fit onto a clothing label and its overall look had
to be high-end and elegant.

Designers considered the materials Nicholson
used in her fashions and developed a palette of
lavender and green to serve as the backdrop for
the logo, which is a feathered arrow that works as
the "f" in her name as it enters the target—the
"o" in Nicholson. The image conveyed is whimsi-
cal, feminine and upscale.

*"We wanted to introduce fresh ideas with
new materials—paper, inks, dies, foil, etc."*

ALLI NEIMAN

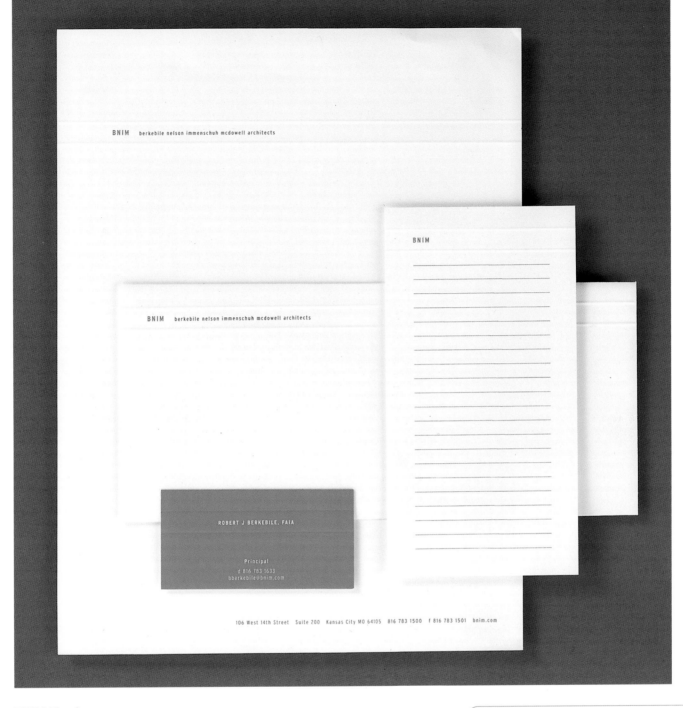

BNIM Identity

Studio: Willoughby Design Group
Art Director: Ann Willoughby
Designer: Nicole Satterwhite
Client: BNIM Architects
Paper: Environment
Colors: two match colors
Special Technique: Horizontal score on all pieces used as a design element

BNIM Architects was relocating to a new building and the time was right for a new identity system. Because the firm is committed to green architecture, designers used recycled materials and kept the design simple, using a horizontal score as the primary design element.

TIP

Get inspired by browsing various books and publications. Then, move on with a sketchpad. Using your computer to get your start inhibits the initial brainstorming process.

Idol Ideas Identity

Studio: Visual Dialogue
Art Director: Fritz Klaetke
Designers: Fritz Klaetke, Ian Varrassi
Client: Idol Ideas
Paper: Fox River Starwhite Vicksburg
Colors: two match colors
Print Run: 500
Special Techniques: Letterpress print-
    ing; business cards and postcards
    die cut into a cloud shape

"We used the thought bubble and
'sky's the limit' imagery to suggest
the process of idea generation and
brainstorming," says Fritz Klaetke,
designer, of this stationery for a
marketing consultancy. "The challenge was to create a memorable
identity that said 'creativity.' Once
people get the business card, they
don't forget it."

*"Don't look for your inspira-
tion in this book. Start
thinking about the client's
key objectives and let the
final form come out of that
content."*

FRITZ KLAETKE

Ideograma Identity

Studio: Ideograma
Art Director: Juan Carlos Fernández
Designer: Susanne Ortiz

Ideograma is a Mexican consultancy firm that "captures ideas floating in the air" so they can be shaped through outstanding corporate identities.

Juan Carlos Fernández, art director on the project, explains, "To communicate that we are a transparent, flexible and innovative firm, we literally took our own definition of 'creators of global identity' and developed an identity with multiple symbols. We used a green balloon (globo, in Spanish) and transformed it into different animals that convey the personality of the application they represent."

This way, a hummingbird is in charge of pollinating prospects in the business card, and a green horse leads a pack of multicolored animals in client communications.

Fernández adds, "Another positive attribute of our identity is that it can be used to explain our creative work method to the clients, illustrated with the process of inflating and giving shape and life to a balloon."

"We are enemies of applying logos like rubber-stamps: each communication piece possesses a specific personality and function, and in the whole they tell us a story."

JUAN CARLOS FERNÁNDEZ

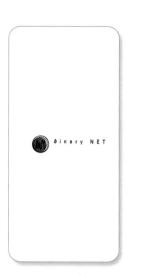

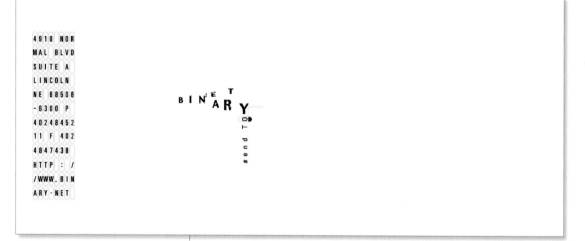

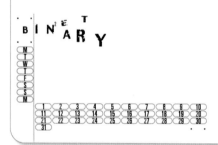

Binary Net Identity

Studio: Archrival, Inc.
Art Director/Designer: Randall Myers
Client: Binary Net

The client's relationship with its customer base and the term "binary" provided the inspiration designer Randall Myers needed to create this identity for an Internet service provider. "Rather than pursuing the obvious direction that has inundated us with zeros and ones, I chose to focus on binary stars," says Myers. "A binary star is a system of two stars that revolve around each other under mutual gravitation."

"The initial challenge was distancing the name from a more common application of the name *binary* while still communicating the idea of code," he says. "The established hierarchy of the number two became important to communicate cooperation and partnership between client and vendor."

"The system must work on more than one level for the client. It needs to address the personality and wide range of services offered. When working on technology-based systems, I think it's important to focus additional attention on more organic elements that can support the overall theme of the system."

RANDALL MYERS

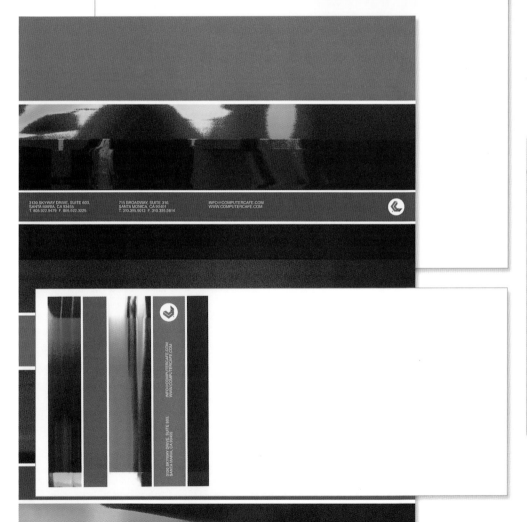

Computer Café Identity

Studio: Segura, Inc.
Art Director: Carlos Segura
Designer: Tnop
Client: Computer Café
Colors: four-color process
Print Run: 10,000

Computer Café is a special effects company. As such, art director Carlos Segura created a 'dreamy' scenery effect as artwork to apply to all the identity components. The challenge was to reflect the high standards of the special effects produced by his client so the print identity would mirror the quality and integrity of Computer Café's work. The result is "very sophisticated and unified," says Segura.

A successful identity is both innovative and flexible. This system uses the logo in a variety of ways—both print and online—while keeping the overall look consistent and memorable.

TIP

First, answer these questions. How do your clients want to position themselves within their market? What are their key differentiators and value propositions? What is their marketing strategy? Get inside their heads. What makes them tick? Where are their visions, hopes and dreams? Once you have all this information, study it, absorb it, and throw it away.

The Big Ticket Identity

Studio: McArtor Design
Art Director/Designer: Jason McArtor
Client: The Big Ticket AM 940
Paper: French Construction Whitewash
Colors: two match colors

The Big Ticket, a sports radio station, gets a retro treatment in the identity created by McArtor Design. AM 940 looks like it has stepped out of

1940 thanks to the designer's choice of type and bold orange and black color palette. "An identity needed to be created to cut through the clutter in the local radio market," says Jason McArtor, art director/designer. "We crafted a logo and identity that would portray the essence of the product—hard-hitting sports radio.

"The design creates an instant impression of sports, which is what the client is. All sports, all the time."

"Corporate design does not have to be boring. All design opportunities have potential. Whether you're doing work for a bank, a law firm or a radio station, come up with a strong concept and execute a quality piece from there."

JASON MCARTOR

The English Channel Identity

Studio: Sunspots Creative, Inc.
Art Director: Rick Bonelli
Designers: Deena Hartley, Rick Bonelli
Client: The English Channel
Paper: Classic Crest Bright White 60 lb., black custom envelopes
Colors: One-color printing with screen tints throughout
Print Run: 1,000
Total Printing Cost: $2,000
Special Techniques: One-color printing to contain costs; screen tints; special glue-on addition of an actual guitar pick

The English Channel specializes in collecting and selling rare British rock music records and artifacts and conducts most of its business at trade shows and through overseas correspondence. The client wanted her prospective customers to feel immediately at ease, so designers decided to attach a guitar pick to the business cards and letterhead as a means to jump-start conversations.

"We developed the playful line of 'pick through your stuff...' to accompany the placement of the pick. The result: everyone who gets the card or letterhead is immediately surprised and finds humor in it."

"We do our research, but we also try to avoid getting too scientific about it. Sometimes we go with gut instincts when it comes to deciding what would make that company speak in the voice they want."

RICK BONELLI

UNCOVER SELF-PROMOTION
secrets

FON .402 4 3 5 2 5 2 5
FAX .402 4 3 5 8 9 3 7
+
INFO@ARCHRIVAL.COM

N 0 1

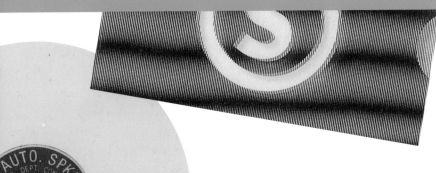

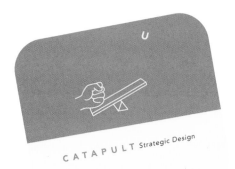

Think. Feel. Work.

PROMOTE YOURSELF, YOUR COMPANY, YOUR TALENT, YOUR FIRM. > > > > > >

Ask any designer what his or her most challenging project is, and they will respond without hesitation: "Designing for yourself." It's true. For designers (and others), being able to objectively focus upon what they do best is no easy feat. Even once they have the direction, it is no easier to choose a look. The problem is that it's so tempting to try everything! It's enticingly easy to want to integrate all the colors, techniques and leading edge design looks that clients would never allow in their identities.

However, if you use all these cool new elements, the curse of the design world may fall on you: your piece may become over-designed, and the resulting identity won't make any sense. Walking the narrow line between quiet restraint and experimenting with that one big opportunity to showcase your capabilities is difficult, but not impossible. The designers showcased in this book have risen to the challenge. And while they all say this project was among their toughest, you wouldn't know it from the fantastic results on the following pages.

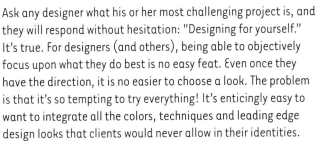

CATAPULT Strategic Design

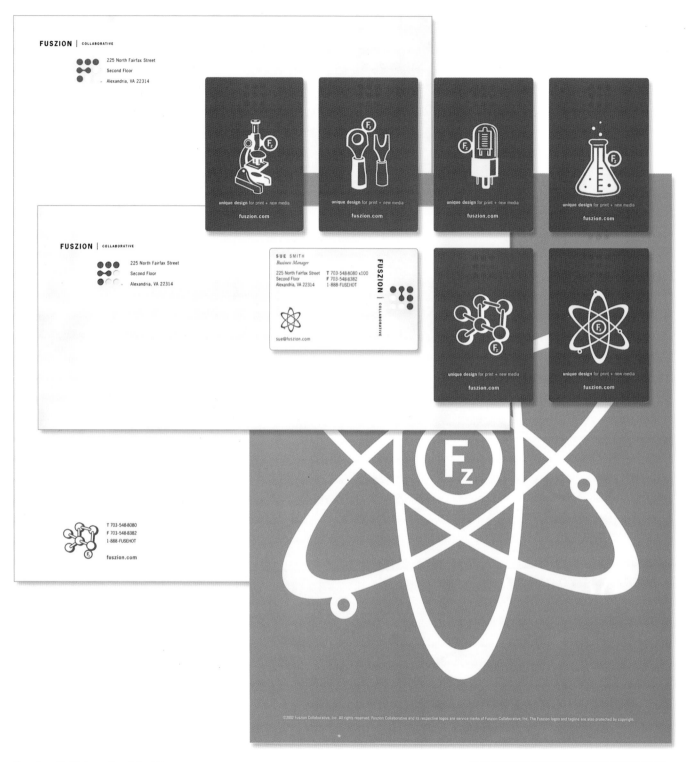

©2002 Fuszion Collaborative, Inc. All rights reserved. Fuszion Collaborative and its respective logos are service marks of Fuszion Collaborative, Inc. The Fuszion logos and tagline are also protected by copyright.

Fuszion Collaborative Identity

Studio: Fuszion Collaborative
Art Directors: Rick Heffner, Tony Fletcher
Designer: Tony Fletcher
Colors: two match colors

On the fifth anniversary of the company's launch, Fuszion Art + Direction announced its name change to Fuszion Collaborative, a name that more accurately reflects its cross-media mindset and philosophy of synergy and cooperation. The name change called for a logo update to reflect the firm's vast creative services, which run from producing print collateral to web design.

The new identity uses six different icons, which are shown on the front and the back of business cards—and letterhead—along with the tagline "unique design for print + new media."

> TIP
>
> *Make the type very readable: Even if five point type looks really cool, nine point type is just as effective.*

Norman Design Identity

Studio: Norman Design
Designers: Armin Vit, Claudit Renzi
Paper: French Paper Smartwhite
Colors: five match colors
Print Run: 1,000
Special Techniques: Printed letterpress on one side of business cards and offset on the other; one each of four different colors printed on the back of every piece

When the time came to redesign its letterhead package, Norman Design wanted to revitalize its identity while reflecting its bold but sophisticated approach to design. Designers also wanted to somehow show their diverse backgrounds, so they decided to use four different colors rather than limiting their image to just one or two "corporate" colors. "Inspiration came from trying to avoid being one more design firm with a terrible logo," says Armin Vit, designer.

"After a few rounds of ideas, we knew we wanted letterpress. Getting it done was another challenge," recalls Vit. To that end, designers gave themselves deadlines and stuck with them; procrastinating wasn't an option.

"This identity system works because of the hierarchy of the information in each piece, the information is clearly placed," says Vit. "The colors are very energetic and that's one of the things we wanted to communicate. The logo represents our simplicity and the belief that less is more."

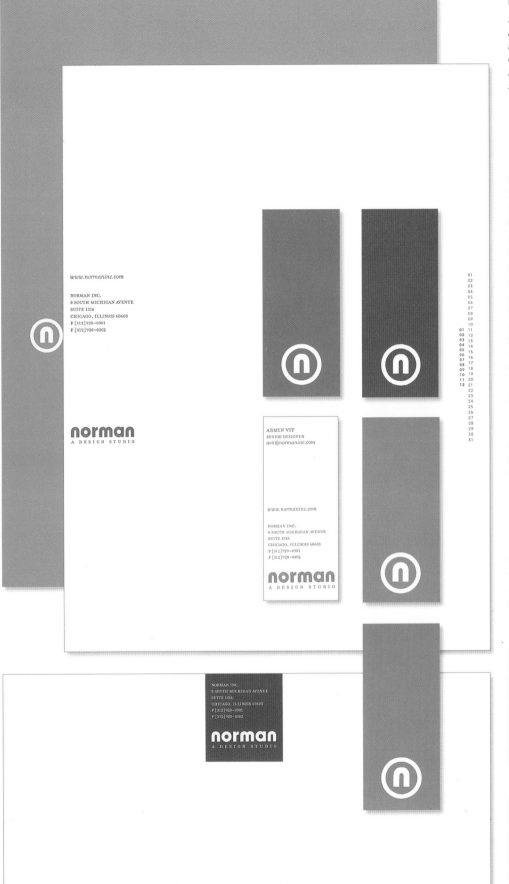

> "We wanted to utilize ideas and printing methods that none of our clients ever want to use."
>
> ARMIN VIT

TIP

Set a strict schedule when designing for yourself, and stick to it! You'll thank yourself.

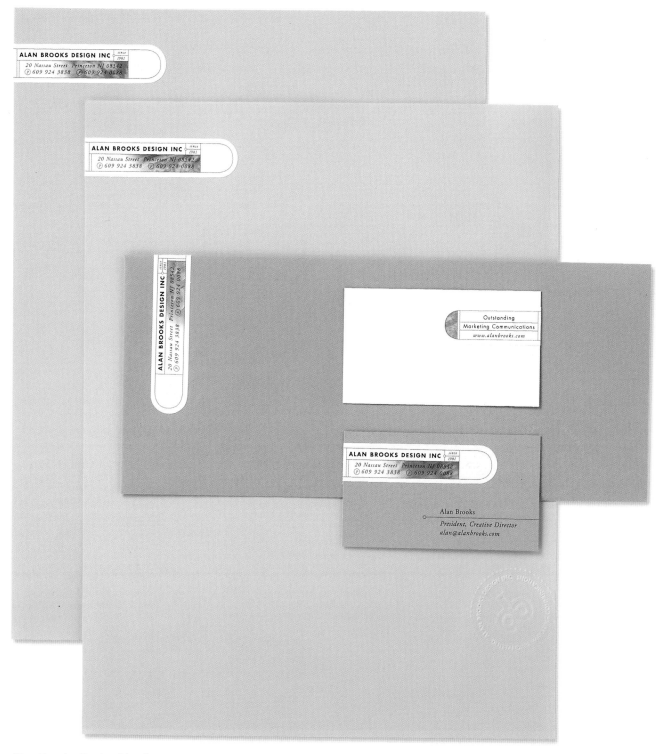

Alan Brooks Design Identity

Studio: Alan Brooks Design Inc.
Art Director/Designer: Alan Brooks
Paper: Neenah Classic Crest
Colors: four-color process
Special Techniques: Embossed, die-cut four-color
　　stickers

Embossed stickers printed in four-color process
distinguish this identity from the rest. The labels

wrap around the business card, mailing envelope
and letterhead, conveying the company name,
logo and contact information on one side and
the firm's web site address and tagline, "Outstanding Marketing Communications," on the
other. The choice of paper stock—a sage green—
adds another color.

　　"It is an inexpensive approach to a complete
identity system," says Alan Brooks.

*"Do everything differently from the
standard conventions."*

ALAN BROOKS

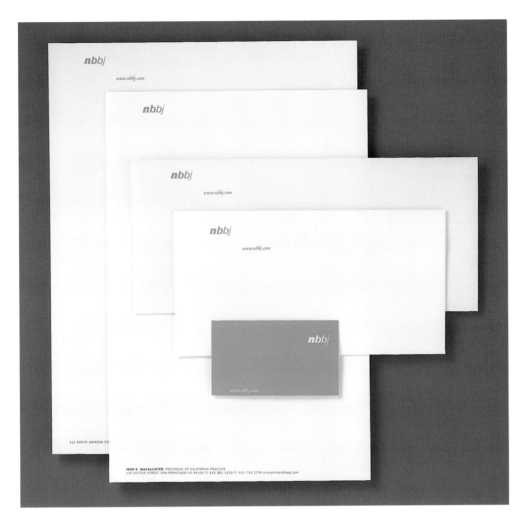

NBBJ Identity

Studio: NBBJ Graphic Design
Art Director: Roddy Grant
Designers: Roddy Grant, Leo Raymundo, Yachun Peng, Eric LeVine, Mark Sanders
Paper: New Leaf Everest White, various weights
Colors: two-over-three (black, Pantone orange, and Pantone 877)

Clean and simple—that's the best description of this identity for NBBJ Graphic Design. The firm serves more than twenty markets and carries out business in a number of applications, so the identity had to be versatile enough to speak to everyone. This one does. Its minimalist design (using 100% post-consumer content recycled materials), clean type (ITC Franklin Gothic and Adobe Garamond), and gray, black and orange color palette speaks on a professional level to any audience.

One might think that such a clean identity would be stodgy, but it's far from it. The rubber-band closure, upscale folder and silver mailing envelope keep this package from looking staid.

> **TIP**
>
> *Think before you design. Don't approach a project as if it's a blank canvas that needs to be decorated. Make a strong statement that will stand out from the everyday piles of paper.*

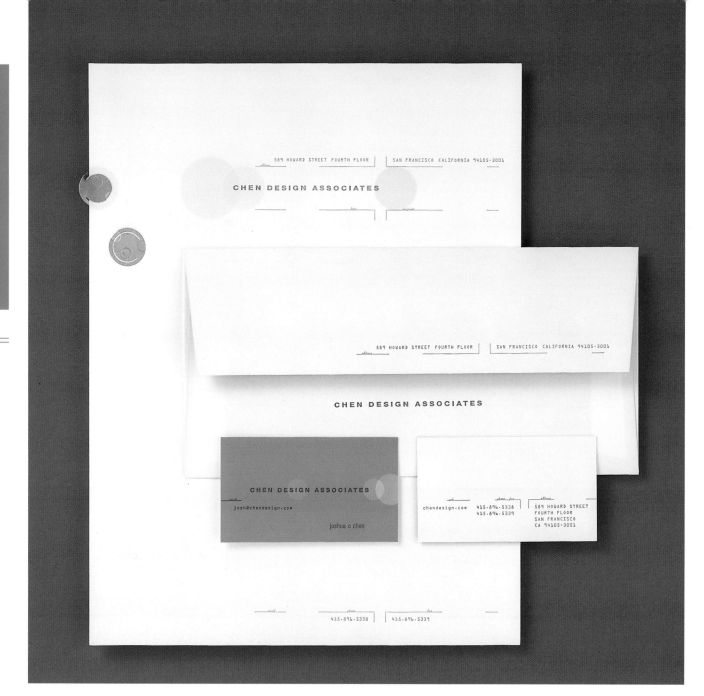

Chen Design Associates Identity

Studio: Chen Design Associates
Art Director: Joshua C. Chen
Designer: Leon Yu
Paper: letterhead—Mohawk Superfine Text and Cover;
   business card—Crane's Kid Finish 130 double-
   thick cover
Print Run: letterhead—5,000; *second sheet*—2,000;
   business cards—2,500
Cost Per Unit: $1.40
Special Techniques: Letterpress and offset printing;
   debossing

"We wanted to express visually...the CDA working philosophy," says Joshua Chen of his identity system. "Simplicity, elegance, boldness, timeless-ness, movement and intersection of ideas were some of the concepts behind this design. The identity carries through to our physical studio space as well as our online presence."

Chen says, "Each person on the staff explored their individual philosophies of design, and we presented these on oversized 'attitude boards,' a collage of type, photos, 3D items, random designed elements, things that communicate who we are and what has influenced us."

Designers in charge of the project distilled everyone's input. "What resulted was all of these values, themes and philosophies boiled down to the barest elements, resulting in the finished product," says Chen.

"The biggest challenge in designing an identity system for your own firm is trying to be objective in the process."

JOSHUA CHEN

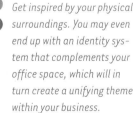

John Korinko Identity

Studio: John Korinko Design
Art Directors: John Korinko, Paula
   Korinko
Paper: Champion Benefit Oyster, Fox
   River Confetti
Colors: three match colors
Special Technique: Application of
   metal eyelets to cards and
   notepads; die-cut corners of
   letterhead, cards and labels;
   spot color background printed
   on label stock to match paper

A new studio called for a new identity system for John Korinko
Design. Physical aspects of the new
office space provided the inspiration for the redesigned image,
including the color palette and ref-
erences to architectural elements—even the touches of metal.
This green and burgundy system is
different yet elegant and distin-
guished, but it didn't come easy.

"The biggest challenge in
designing for yourself is creating
something that you can live with
for a long time," says John Korinko,
art director. To get over this hurdle,
designers approached the job as
though they were the client. They
defined the objectives and made
sure that the final design satisfied
all the agreed upon goals.

In the end, it all came together—the identity reflects the firm's
work environment and design style.
"If you receive our stationery and
then visit our studio, you'll feel like
you've been here before," says
Korinko.

TIP

*Get inspired by your physical
surroundings. You may even
end up with an identity system that complements your
office space, which will in
turn create a unifying theme
within your business.*

Catapult Identity

Studio: Catapult Strategic Design
Art Director/Designer: Art Lofgreen
Colors: four match colors
Print Run: 2,000

How many ways can you catapult something into the air? This stationery provides the answer via multiple line art illustrations on different colored versions of the business card, mailing label, envelope and letterhead. The illustrations are clever and they tie the firm's name together nicely with what it does.

"The challenge was to show catapulting in an unexpected way that related to what we do as designers," says Art Lofgreen, art director. "The hands convey the idea of craftsmanship. This works well for us. Our clients expect something unusual from a design firm."

 TIP

Force yourself to fill at least ten pages of your sketchbook with thumbnails before taking a rough idea to the next step of refinement.

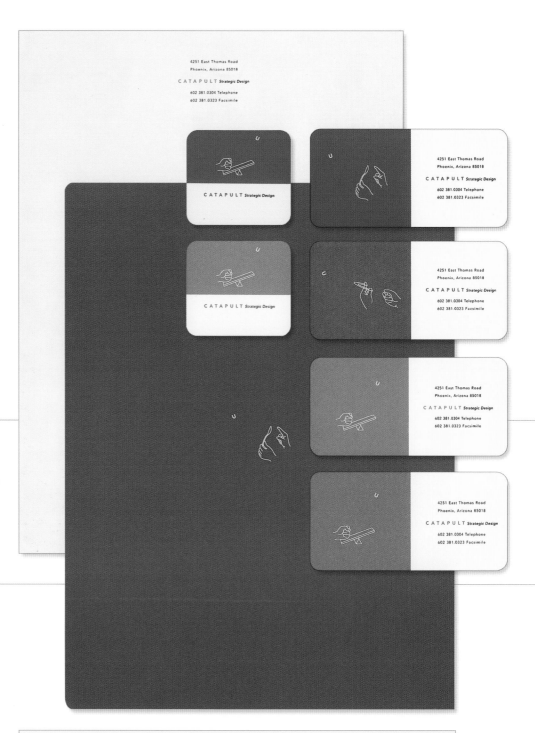

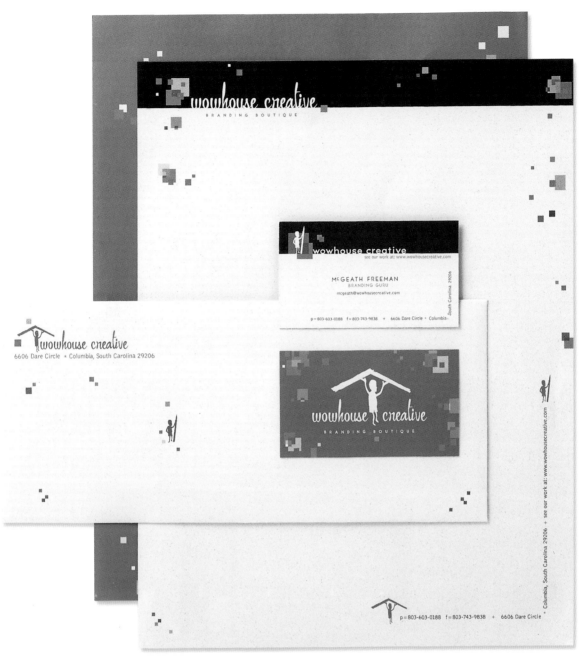

Wowhouse Creative Identity

Studio: Wowhouse Creative
Art Director: McGeath Freeman
Designer: Andie Freeman
Paper: Fox River Crushed Leaf Silver Sparkles 80 lb.
  text and 110 lb. cover
Colors: two-over-one (using process black and PMS
  8265 metallic)
Print Run: letterhead—1,000; envelopes—1,000;
  business cards—500
Cost Per Unit: $.60

Wowhouse Creative was moving to a new office and expanding, and needed no better reason to produce a new logo. Designers opted to lose everything from the old identity except the studio's name. Their goal: to develop a system that would be comfortable for conservative clients while attracting more adventurous prospects.

For inspiration, they turned to their physical office space and artistic background. "The squares are reminiscent of the light through our picture window and the primitive logo figure are inspired by the art in our office," says Andie Freeman, designer. The black bar anchors the design and allows plenty of white space for readability.

"The metallic ink, the square, the figure and the silver sparkles are elements that add life and movement to the system," adds Freeman. "This system works because it simply and clearly tells the Wowhouse story."

"Identity is just another communicating device. So communicate!"

ANDIE FREEMAN

Platinum Design Business Card

Studio: Platinum Design, Inc.
Creative Director: Vickie Peslak
Art Director: Mike Jayle
Designer: Andy Taray
Colors: two match colors plus metallic
Size: $2^{1}/_{4}$" x $3^{1}/_{2}$"
Special Production Technique: A laser was used to
    die cut fine "shards" into the card

"The challenge was to print and die cut pieces
that were extreme, and to be cost-efficient at the
same time," says Vickie Peslak, creative director.
To achieve the fine die cut required of this
design—rays emanating from the logo—laser
die-cutting was a necessity.

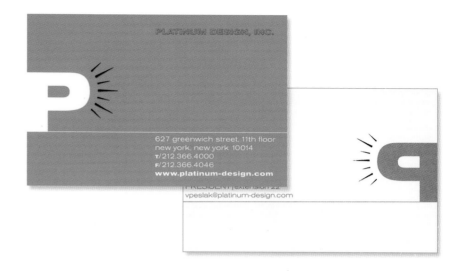

K. Kargl Graphic Design Business Card

Studio: K. Kargl Graphic Design
Designer: Kathleen Weil Kargl
Paper: Cougar Opaque Smooth
Colors: two match colors
Print Run: 500

This freelancer was sketching for a client when
she came up with this idea for herself. The design
is simply constructed using a two-color palette.
By creating a stamped effect for the initial "K"
and by using the only half of a self-portrait, this
card is singularly unique.

Morris Creative Business Cards

Studio: Morris Creative, Inc.
Art Director: Steven Morris
Designer: Tom Davie
Paper: Fox River Sundance Warm White, smooth
Colors: five match colors plus spot varnish
Print Run: 5,000
Cost Per Unit: Nothing, the studio traded design
    services

These business cards look more like coasters than
traditional business cards—and that's exactly
what the designer intended. Designers used a
round die and perforations so it can be cut or torn
away on the dotted line and used as a coaster.

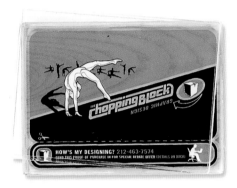

The Chopping Block Business Cards

Studio: The Chopping Block, Inc.
Designers: Rob Reed, Matthew Richmond, Tom Romer
Client: The Chopping Block, Inc.
Colors: four-color process over four match colors
Print Run: 1,000

"We needed to come up with a creative, offbeat solution for our self promo that could be easily updated if needed," says Rob Reed, one of the designers who tackled this project. "A pack of unbound cards was the perfect solution."

The cards double as business cards and promotional pieces. Many graphic design companies offer a series of cards; however, this firm goes a step further and actually encourages recipients to collect the entire set.

"The Chopping Block is known for doing things a little differently, so our identity needed to be handled in the same way: over-the-top but smart," says Reed.

> "Do something you've never seen before. There's so much stuff floating around out there you really need to create a smart, unique solution that is memorable."
>
> ROB REED

Graphics Factory Identity System

Studio: Graphics Factory
Art Director: Lance Saeger
Paper: Wausau, Royal Bond Natural, Light Cockle
Colors: two match colors
Print Run: 2,000

This studio was renamed and consequently needed to refresh its graphics. The challenges were to find an identity that utilized the equity built by the previous image, and produce it within a very short two-week time frame.

Designers chose to keep the gear icon and typefaces from the previous identity but updated them for the new package, thereby maintaining the recognition factor that the original design built over its sixteen years of use. Then they added the bar code over the telephone numbers to communicate the firm's strong retail background.

"By distressing the name and including elements such as the bar code and the gear, this system successfully represents a retail business that resides in the warehouse district of Minneapolis," says Lance Saeger, art director.

TIP

Ask questions. You can never have too much information!

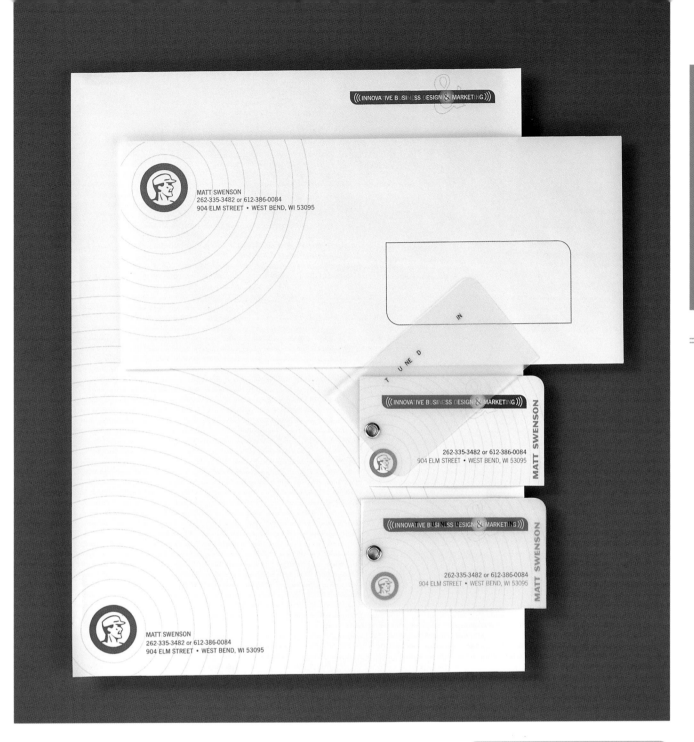

Matt Swenson Identity

Studio: Matt Swenson Design & Marketing
Designer: Matt Swenson
Paper: letterhead/envelopes—Cougar Opaque;
    business card—C2S KromeKote and Neenah UV
    Ultra Radiant White Translucent
Colors: letterhead system—two match colors;
    business cards—four-color process over two spot
    colors and one spot overlay
Print Run: 1,000
Special Technique: Four-color backer shines
    through a printed plastic overlay attached with
    a grommet; custom corner die cuts; embossing

"I viewed my own identity as more than just a way
to provide clients and prospects with my phone
number and address," says Matt Swenson, designer. "I wanted it to be a conversation-starter that
would open the door for me so I could give my 30-
second pitch."

"The four-color backer represents all the
noise and static we as marketers must try to
break through in order to successfully deliver our
messages. The service I can provide is to help my
clients get 'tuned in' to what sets them apart
from the competition and to what their customers
need and want—a message I convey on the printed plastic overlay," Swenson adds.

In fact, when the recipient slides the overlay
away from the card, it carries a singular message
in black type: *Tuned In*.

> "A system's elements should have
> some positive meaning behind them,
> yet they should also reflect the com-
> pany in a way that allows for shifts in
> meaning over time, as the company
> grows and changes."
>
> MATT SWENSON

Archrival Identity

Studio: Archrival, Inc.
Art Director: Clint! Runge
Designers: Clint! Runge, Ryan Cooper,
Charles Hull
Colors: four-color process, plus one
spot color
Print Run: 1,250

"Our firm's system was derived from many of the same concepts found in the great novel *Moby Dick*, only in this case, it seems it is our passion for good design that keeps us up late at night, weekend after weekend, 'tormented by an everlasting itch for things remote.'"

"Just as the character Ishmael can see the use of objects for more than just their intended use, our studio staff of architects, graphic designers, artists and advertisers work together in solving problems from multiple viewpoints," says Clint! Runge of Archrival's identity system.

The look is eclectic and deliberately vague as some elements are purposely faded and its minimal copy is smudged and blurred. This special effect was achieved by copying fax illustrations multiple times.

"Focus more on great ideas and less on visual executions. You can always get better at design executions, but if your design is based on static, blah ideas, the design will never achieve that level of a truly great system. I too often see young designers trying to impress through their ability to use software... I'm more frequently impressed by designers who can use those tools to execute a great idea."

CLINT! RUNGE

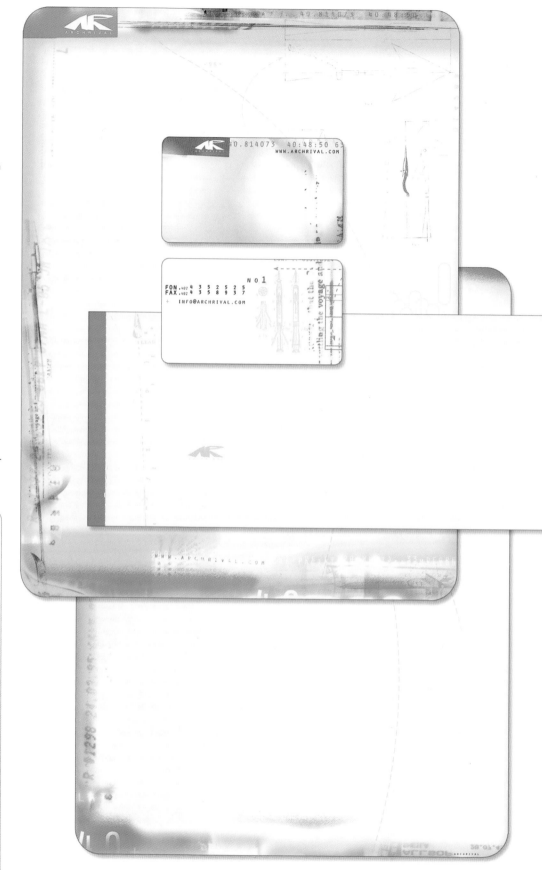

Cave Images Identity

Studio: Cave Images
Designers: David Edmundson, Matt Cave
Paper: letterhead/envelope—Fox River Starwhite; *business card*—Potlatch McCoy Silk
Colors: four-color process plus match colors
Print Run: letterhead/envelope—1,000; *brochures*—500
Special Technique: Spot gloss varnish on business cards

Cave Images wanted an identity that positioned the studio as an upscale firm with a creative focus without appearing overdesigned, so its identity could act as a harmonious complement to the work the firm would most often showcase.

The result is an identity based on a palette of four colors and copy that talks about finding your "visual voice." The folding business card, in particular, shows the studio's mindset and creative approach to design. Its brochure is easily customized for the recipient, while not appearing flimsy. Its brushed metal cover is impressive, as is the work featured inside.

> "An identity should connect with people on an emotional level to create an enduring impression."
>
> MATT CAVE

Sleeping Dragon Identity

Studio: Sleeping Dragon Graphics, LLC
Art Director/Designer: Laura Moberly
Paper: Weyerhaeuser Cougar, Beckett Enhance
Colors: two match colors
Print Run: 2,000
Cost Per Unit: $.33
Special Technique: Die-cut business cards

This designer really liked the sage green envelope she specified for her system, but was fearful that it might be discontinued, so she had the studio's return address printed on a wraparound label. If the color eventually is discontinued, the firm will merely choose another envelope without having to go back on press.

"This works because everything works together to get people's attention and to keep this company in their thoughts," says designer Laura Moberly.

"Combine the visual and the verbal to express the uniqueness of the company."

LAURA MOBERLY

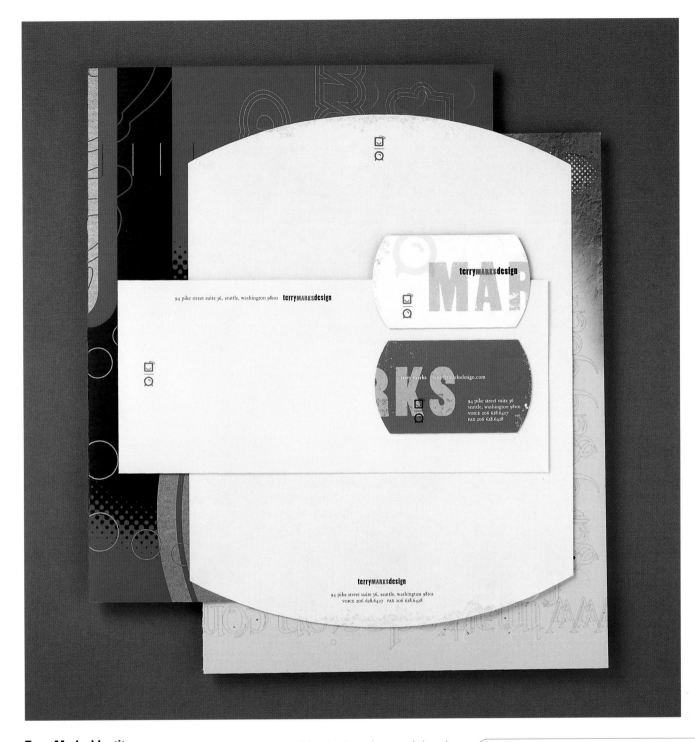

Terry Marks Identity

Studio: Terry Marks Design
Art Director: Terry Marks
Designers: Terry Marks, Josh Michels
Paper: letterhead/envelope—French Dur-o-Tone
    Butcher White 80 lb. text; business card—
    Muscletone Construction Cover 140 lb.
Colors: three-over-three match colors
Print Run: letterhead—1,000; business cards—500
Cost Per Unit: business card—$.35; letterhead—$.66;
    envelope—$.50
Special Techniques: Engraving; die cut; spiked varnish

Designers of this identity package say their goal was to achieve a balance between two extremes—"the rough" and "the refined" of who they are and the work they do. Sounds tough, but not for this team. "We bounced a few things back and forth until we had something we were happy with," says Terry Marks. "This system reflects the collaboration and personalities that make up Terry Marks Design."

"Don't overanalyze or try to convey too much. It's a small piece of real estate to communicate a whole lot. Simple ideas stay with people."

TERRY MARKS

Osborn Identity

Studio: Osborn
Art Director: Juliette Bellocq
Paper: Cranes Crest 100% Cotton,
    French Paper
Colors: four match colors
Print Run: letterhead—8,500; *business
    cards*—7500; *envelopes*—2,500
Cost Per Unit: letterhead—$.31; *busi-
    ness cards*—$.20; *envelopes*—$.175

Osborn, a graphic design firm that
also specializes in architecture and
construction management, wanted an
identity that would reflect the firm's
history and new direction. The firm
offers an array of services and there
exist many differences among the
personalities, interests and expertise
of the personnel. "Creative tension, in
a modular system, became the main
inspiration point for this project," says
Juliette Bellocq, art director.

Consequently, the identity was
developed on a series of superimposed
grids that create infinite pattern possibilities and a sense of space. "The
fabrics created eventually become
typographic grids or patterns from the
most ordered to the most asynchro-
nous. We are exploring regularity and
tension, unpredictability and preci-
sion," says Bellocq. These patterns are
played out in eight different ways on
the backs of eight business cards, all
of which are given to each employee.

The typographic logo provides
enough flexibility for each department
to use on a wide variety of documents.
"It is a mix of rectangular and supple
shapes, very legible at small scale and
revealing its typographic details when
used on architecture scale graphics,"
adds Bellocq.

Does it work? "In our case, the
color palette and the range of business card backs are triggering reac-
tions and questions," Bellocq says. "It
becomes an opportunity to introduce
the story of our firm and the diversity
of our office."

TIP

*Make sure you spend just
as much time researching
the company and thinking
about the objective as you
do executing the ideas.*

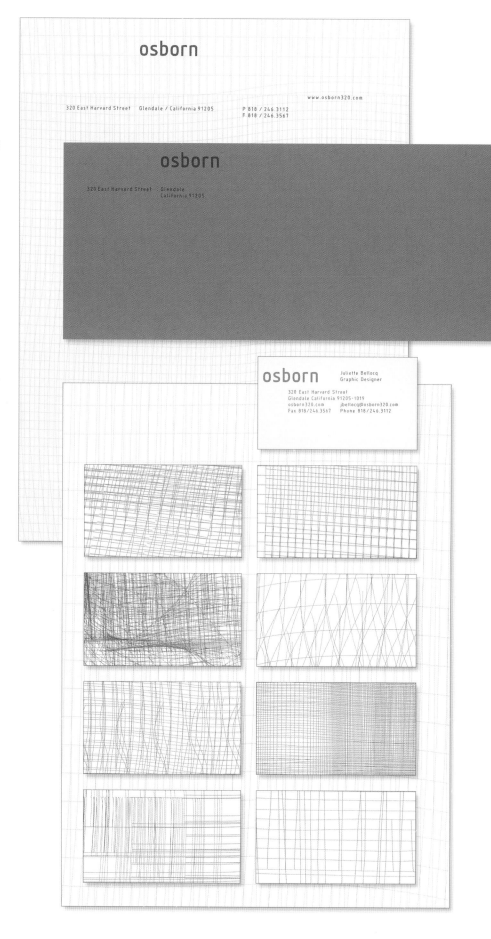

Segura Identity

Studio: Segura, Inc.
Art Director/Designer: Carlos Segura
Colors: four-color process
Print Run: 5,000
Special Techniques: Plastic business cards; custom
    converted envelope; six individual backs with
    different artwork on each

Carlos Segura wanted to showcase the variety of
his studio's work without being too specific, so he
designed a system where each item has one of six
different pieces of artwork printed on the back.
"It is a wonderful feature and gallery of what we
do for a living," says Segura.

The small, lowercase type treatment does not
detract from but calls attention to the artwork,
which is colorful and multi-faceted like an
abstract painting.

TIP

*Get on paper mills' mailing lists so you're
sure to get samples of all the latest
papers. Ask your local paper merchant for
a sample box containing swatch books for
the mills it represents.*

HLL Logo

Studio: Epoxy Communication, Inc.
Art Directors: George Fok, Daniel
 Fortin
Designer: George Fok
Client: HLL clothing

Gourmet Soiree Logo

Art Director/Designer: Scott Boylston
Client: Savannah, GA chapter of the
 American Red Cross—Gourmet
 Soiree was a fundraiser

SiSU Logo

Studio: SiSU Design
Art Director/Designer: Jennifer Stucker

Vintage Couture Logo

Studio: [i]e design
Art Director: Marcie Carson
Designers: Cya Nelson
Client: Jennifer Nicholson/Pearl,
 high-end clothing store

Yourteamsucks.com Logo

Studio: Gunter Advertising
Art Director/Designer: Randy Gunter
Client: Idian.com, entertainment web
 site provider

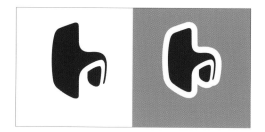

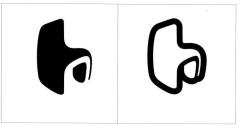

OBF Logo

Studio: Hiestand Design
Art Director: Lisa Buchanan
Designers: Lisa Buchanan, Britney Barren
Client: Oxford Bible Fellowship Church

Race the Bear Logo

Studio: X Design Company
Art Director/Designer: Alex Valderrama
Client: Race the Bear Mountain Bike Challenge

Café Toluca Logo

Studio: Catapult Strategic Design
Art Director: Art Lofgreen, Peter Jones
Designer: Peter Jones
Client: Café Toluca, upscale Mexican fast food restaurant

Rice n' Roll Logo

Studio: Monster Design
Art Directors: Hannah Wygal, Theresa Veranth
Designer: Theresa Veranth
Client: Rice n' Roll, a fast food sushi franchise

Pureburn Logo

Studio: 344 Design, LLC/Modernista
Art Director: Gary Koepke
Designer: Stefan G. Bucher
Client: Roxio, CD burning software

Gunnar Swanson Identity

Studio: Gunnar Swanson Design Office
Art Director/Designer: Gunnar Swanson
Paper: letterhead—Gilbert Esse; *envelope*—Brown Kraft; *business cards*—French Construction Cement Green
Colors: letterhead—two match colors, *envelope/business cards*—three-over-two; *mailing labels*—four-color process on ink-jet printer
Special Techniques: Letterpress printing on a small hand press; all design and printing done in-house to minimize costs

When redesigning the studio's letterhead, Gunnar Swanson wanted to emphasize the studio's personal identity. "Clients are buying me and my expertise, not some fictional 'and Associates.' If they wanted a big, impersonal design firm, they'd hire one," says Swanson.

The talking head logo used in the identity ties the printed letterhead into the studio's web site while Swanson used color to achieve variety and unity in the stationery. "The separate features—the talking head logo and the logotype—represent both the strength and the challenge of the system."

Swanson opted for letterpress printing to control the price and impart an earthy, textural quality to the identity. To save some money, Swanson grouped all of the elements together and e-mailed them to a die-making firm that made a letterpress cutout of them. Swanson cut that into smaller elements on a table saw, paying for only one medium-sized letterpress cut instead of many smaller ones.

"An identity needs to be a system, not just a logo to stamp on everything or a color to pour over everything. This means multiple features used systematically but not necessarily without variety. An identity needs to be a visual anchor but not so overwhelming that other communication suffers."

GUNNAR SWANSON

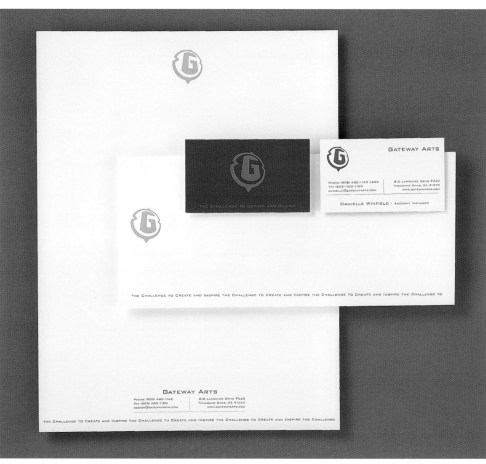

Gateway Arts Identity

Studio: Gateway Arts
Art Director: Dave Carlson
Designer: Dave Ruhr
Paper: folder/business card—Endeavor Velvet 130 lb. cover; *envelope/letterhead*—Top Kote 70 lb. text
Colors: two match colors
Print Run: 2,500
Cost Per Unit: folders—$1.20; *letterhead/envelopes*—$2,000 total; *business cards*—$.35

"The inspiration for this piece came to me when I finally reached the top of Mount Everest, dehydrated and cold. I saw a vision in the sky against the clouds. It was our 'G' logo in a metallic silver color reversed out against a rich, bold deep red color. I knew then that this was meant to be our new stationery design," Dave Carlson, art director, explains facetiously.

To minimize costs without sacrificing a dramatic, bold look, the system is designed to print in two colors—a metallic silver and deep red—on a velvet finish stock. A third black plate was used to drop in names on the business cards.

"We think it is cool, and that's what matters most."

DAVE CARLSON

Structure Communications Identity

Studio: Structure Communications Group, LLC
Art Director: Michael Chinn
Designers: Michael Chinn, Alex Peltekian
Papers: Fox River 24 lb. text, Bright White Wove 88 lb. cover
Colors: three match colors
Print Run: business cards—4 sets of 500; *letterhead, envelopes*—2,000
Cost Per Unit: business cards—$.99; *letterhead*—$.54; *envelopes*—$2.63
Special Techniques: Die-cut envelopes and business cards

Designers admit that the toughest obstacle in creating this system was themselves. "You are your own worst critic and nothing is quite right or good enough," says Michael Chinn, art director. Designers knew what they wanted from the beginning but ended up developing new comps over and over for months in search of something that was dynamic and organic while possessing motion and energy. "We sought an 'Astrofuturis-tico' look—sophisticated elegance with a twist," says Chinn.

"*The inspirations for the design of this piece were Frank G architecture, nature, good grooves, Sasha, Reggae, porn, ganja, Starbucks Venti Lattes, the studio Erector set, the Sci-Fi channel, Reagan National Airport, gummi bears, and James Bond movies.*"

MICHAEL CHINN

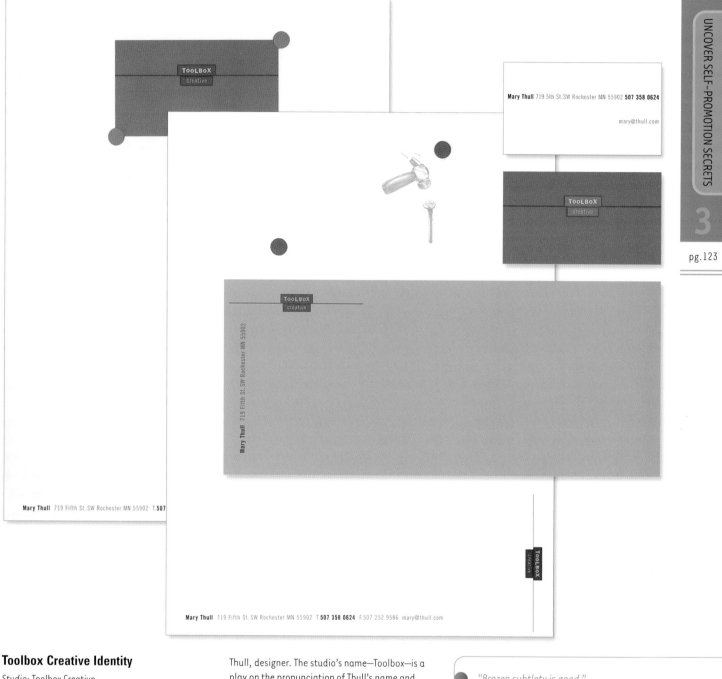

Toolbox Creative Identity

Studio: Toolbox Creative
Designer: Mary Thull
Paper: letterhead—Classic Crest; *envelope*—French
  Forstone; *notecard*—French Speckletone Basics
Colors: two match colors
Print Run: 1,000
Cost Per Unit: $1.30
Special Techniques: Embossed die cuts used for the
  nail heads at the top of letterhead to hold the
  business card in place; gray metallic ink used
  throughout; varnish used over red on the
  business card

"I wanted to design a memorable piece—clever but
not too clever and definitely not cute," says Mary

Thull, designer. The studio's name—Toolbox—is a
play on the pronunciation of Thull's name and,
she fears, too cutesy. Her solution was to develop
an industrial-looking design.

The execution is clever in that the nail heads
are embossed and die cut on the letterhead,
which neatly holds a business card in place without paper clips and works as the stationery's
masthead. Moreover, the red "pops" against the
soft gray color palette.

"This design works for me because people
don't get it right away. Most eventually do," says
Thull. "Any design that catches the eye and makes
a person smile or think for a few moments is nice,"
she adds.

"Brazen subtlety is good."

MARY THULL

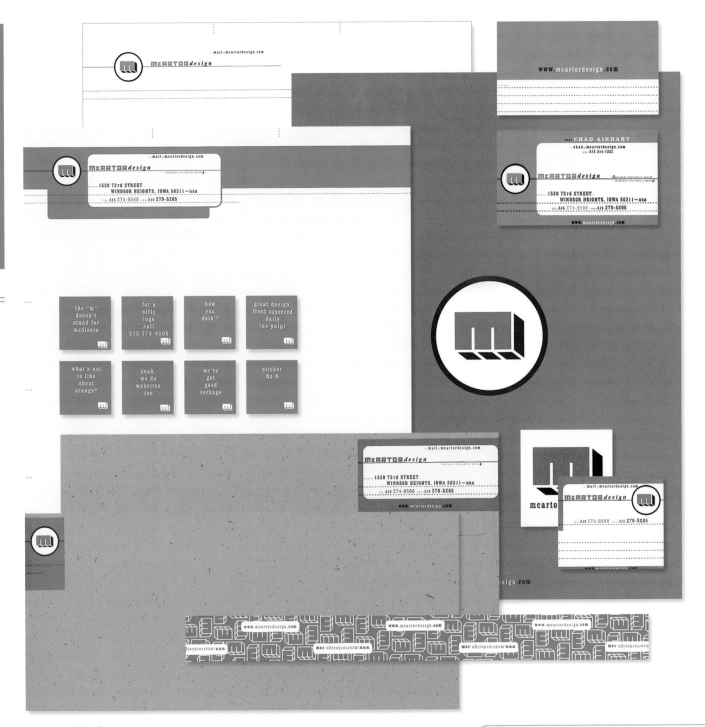

McArtor Identity

Studio: McArtor Design
Art Director/Designer: Jason McArtor
Paper: French Construction White
Colors: two match colors
Print Run: 1,000
Cost Per Unit: $1.00
Special Technique: Stickers were gang-run on a
tabloid size sheet and cut down, eliminating
the need to print envelopes

Jason McArtor wanted to freshen up his firm's
identity system, while maintaining some of the
structure of the original look. He found the
answer in this redesign, which retained the
studio's signature orange color, along with a
layout similar to the old system.

"As our company has grown, we wanted to
appear smarter and more corporate to potential
clients. This identity maintains our fun approach
to the work we do but is cleaner and sleeker than
our previous identity, thus improving our first
impression to a client."

TIP

*Get a good feel for your client's expecta-
tions before jumping into a project
because ultimately the client has the final
say. Develop a strong concept into a solution that you will be able to justify and sell
to the client. Much of this business is
being able to sell what you create, so have
reasons for what you do.*

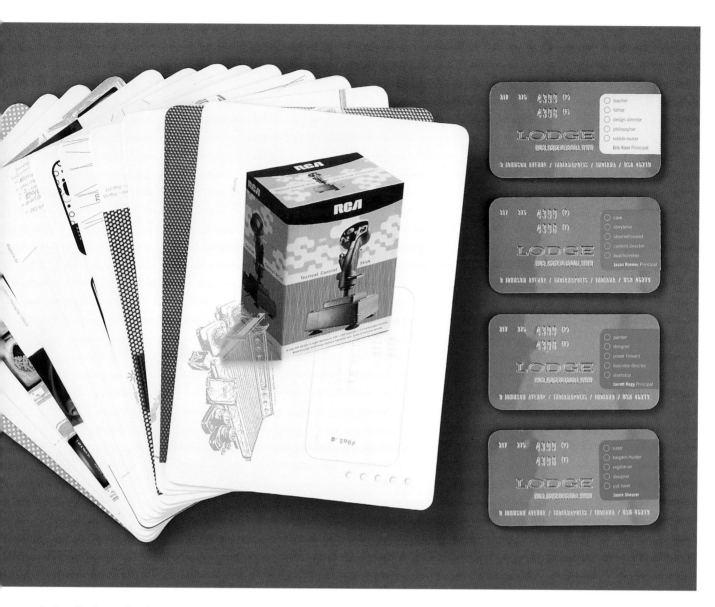

Lodge Business Cards

Studio: Lodge Design Co.
Designer: Eric Kass
Paper: Aluminum
Colors: four match metallics
Print Run: 1,000
Cost Per Unit: $1.00
Special Production Techniques: Aluminum cards are blind embossed with common information, and then customized to the individual with a one-color metallic label

"Our cards cannot be ignored," says Eric Kass. "The type pressed into cold aluminum quickly communicates strength, substance and an industrial-style work ethic."

The cards, Kass says, also are intensely personal. Each has a wrap-around label in a metallic color chosen by the individual. Along with the employee's name are five titles, one of which portrays their role at Lodge Design. The others give information about the employee's personal life, including everything from 'father' to 'storyteller.'

Interestingly, the cards are also stamped into four-color cards that describe recent projects, and are perforated for easy removal.

"The challenge was to represent the company brand with continuity while letting each person express themselves individually," adds Kass. "Our identity works because it is us in the truest sense."

TIP

Explore materials other than paper for your identity system. Think about using fabric, metal, foam, wood, gel, plastic or even food for the next iteration of your identity.

Sagmeister Identity

Studio: Sagmeister, Inc.
Art Director: Stefan Sagmeister
Paper: Strathmore Writing White
Colors: one match
Print Run: 1,000
Special Techniques: Business card is offset printed; foil wraps around card like a slipcase; stationery has an offset printed bellyband

The master of visual illusion, Stefan Sagmeister created this identity system to do something unusual that would represent many of the studio's designs. Playing tricks on the eye is a hallmark of Sagmeister's designs and this creation is no exception.

"We actually got a number of jobs directly through the business card," says Sagmeister.

The challenges were mostly production-oriented. Originally, the pieces were all assembled in-house, which consumed an inordinate amount of time. The second time around, Sagmeister let the printer do the assembly, which proved challenging because of the tight constrictions on trimming and alignment.

"An identity system needs to honestly and elegantly represent the nature of the client's business."

STEFAN SAGMEISTER

Clean Slate Identity

Studio: Clean Slate
Designer: John Lopes
Paper: Mohawk Navajo Brilliant White
    130 lb. cover, 80 lb. text
Colors: stationery and sticker—two
    match colors; *brochure*—four-
    color process
Print Run: 1,000
Cost Per Unit: $.75
Special Production Techniques: Blind
    emboss; die cut; grommets; over-
    printing of two inks to simulate a
    third color

Clean Slate wanted an identity that left no doubt of its name, so that's exactly what the team designed: a clean, smooth white page that is used for everything from letters and invoices to proposals and estimates. The name is blind embossed on the sheet to reinforce the name, but everything isn't white. Showstopping red and black graphics proclaiming the "countless possibilities" are found throughout the system.

"Designing simply and for yourself are two of the biggest challenges," says John Lopes, designer. "The tendency is to want to do it all and say it all when promoting yourself."

TIP

Overprint two inks to simulate a third color.

"Design for your client's message to its audience and if your identity system gets noticed, it's a bonus—but not the goal."

JOHN LOPES

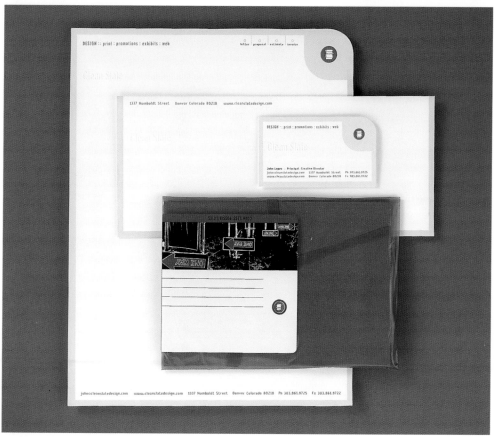

Dotzero Mini Portfolio with Magnifier Business Cards

Studio: Dotzero
Art Directors/Designers: Karen Wippich, Jon Wippich
Paper: Warren Lustro Dull
Colors: four-color process
Print Run: 1,000

This design firm's portfolio is presented on a key ring like business cards, hence the handy inclusion of a magnifier. Logos are presented on one card, business cards on another. Examples of packaging, poster work and even a photograph of collateral pieces are included on the cards. It's a clever, catchy presentation that takes up little space, is easy to mail and is certain not to overwhelm a potential client.

Surprisingly, these cards were actually designed as "labels" to accent an end-of-the-year gift for clients. They were made to be

reversible to get more designs to choose from and any unused cards could be trimmed and used as alternate business cards after the event.

"We wanted a bunch of different looks so clients in the same office would get different bag labels as well as different goodies to trade with," says Jon Wippich, who co-designed the project.

 TIP

Think ahead to see if you can repurpose some piece of your business collateral. That way, you can save money by using one piece in two different ways.

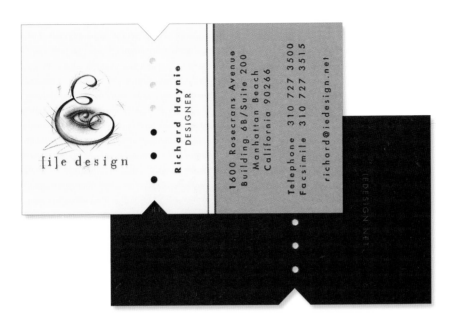

[i]e design Business Card

Studio: [i]e design, Los Angeles
Art Director: Marcie Carson
Designers: Marcie Carson, Cya Nelson, Amy Klass
Paper: Fox River Select 100% Cotton, Warm White
Colors: four-color process plus two match colors

These business cards are die cut and letterpressed for an elegant look that manages to communicate a lot of information on a single side. With more and more business cards using both sides to convey an enormous amount of contact information, this one manages to include it all—along with a logo—in a small amount of space without appearing cluttered.

Mindspin Business Card

Studio: Mindspin Studio
Art Director/Designer: Tanja Neil
Copywriter: Adam Jablonski
Paper: Navajo
Colors: two colors
Print Run: 2,000
Cost Per Unit: $.35

A pattern of swirls in metallic silver characterizes this card for Mindspin Studio. The look is simple and straightforward. The message—"be seen"—is succinctly communicated without ado. It worked for the studio. "As confirmed by the overwhelming client response, the system firmly stands out," says Tanja Neil, art director.

160 over 90 Business Card

Studio: 160 over 90
Art Director/Designer: Martin Duffy
Paper: Strathmore Ultimate White
Colors: three match colors
Print Run: 10,000
Special Techniques: Business card is die cut and includes an embossed label

"160 over 90 is about getting a human reaction," says Martin Duffy, art director. "By creating a system that is rich in texture, using embossing and stickers, we wanted each piece to be felt, touched and examined.

"Because each business card and envelope is handmade using an attached label, how can we assure quality and consistency on every piece? We don't. It is about the human touch—however good or bad."

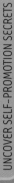

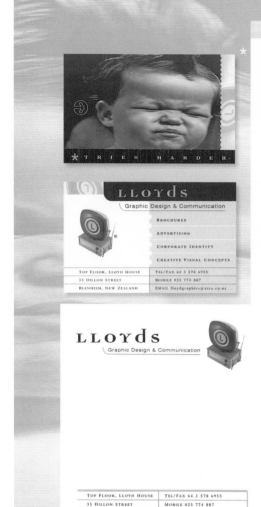

Lloyds Graphic Design & Communication Identity

Studio: Lloyds Graphic Design & Communication
Art Director/Designer: Alexander Lloyd
Paper: Elements Soft White Lines
Colors: two match colors
Print Run: 1,000
Special Technique: Matte lamination

Designers wanted to update the firm's image by introducing a retro TV set into the new identity, a symbol that would communicate the studio's ability to look at high-tech design from a different perspective. The planned identity would be a huge departure from the existing image, so the team decided to launch the makeover at one time rather than replacing pieces as the old identity supplies were used up.

"This system works because of the strength of the TV icon. It works well as a stand-alone, in process or match color, while the careful font choices and fine line work lend an air of craftsmanship and attention to detail. Also, the use of images on the back of all the items gives a humorous, retro twist," says Alexander Lloyd.

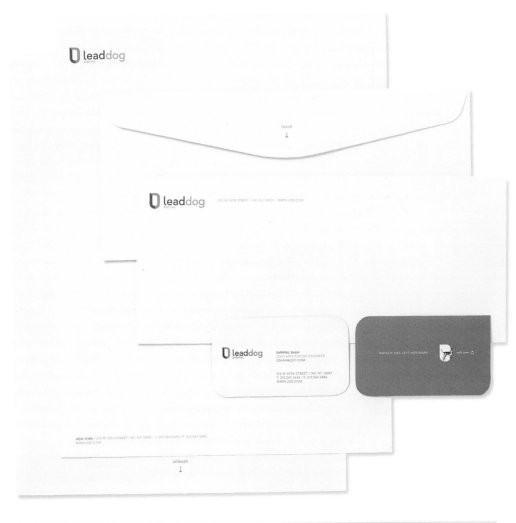

Lead Dog Digital Identity

Studio: Lead Dog Digital
Art Director: Natalie Lam
Designers: Natalie Lam, John Turner, Stacey Geller, Tom Lynch
Colors: stationery and folder—three match colors; *brochure and calendar*—four-color process plus one match color
Print Run: stationery—30 lots of 350 each; *brochure/folder*—700; *calendar*—1,000
Special Techniques: stationery/folder—die cut and embossed; *brochure*—foil stamped

This studio started out as a design boutique where the principals loved their dogs and brought them to work, hence the company's name. Over the years, the studio grew, and it needed a more sophisticated, high-tech image that reflected its full-service capabilities.

All four partners had different backgrounds and perceptions of what they wanted in a new system, so while it was difficult getting an initial consensus, eventually everyone agreed to use the initials of an "L" and "D" to form a unique symbol.

"Getting everyone to agree on one voice and one look and direction for all our branding needs was the biggest challenge," says Natalie Lam. "The result was truly a good reflection of the diverse personalities, youthful energy and friendly culture of the company while staying away from anything too trendy and 'dot-comy.'"

"Don't follow trends; think first. Sketch ideas before executing. Experiment. Avoid stock photography. Don't be too serious. Be provocative."

NATALIE LAM

Strohl Identity

Studio: Pomeroy Dakota
Art Directors: Eric Strohl, Christine Celic
Paper: French Construction
Special Techniques: Components
  printed as needed on the studio
  printer; labels printed on self-
  adhesive stock and then hand-cut

Russian packing labels and national
park signage provided the inspirations for this identity system. Since
there was no budget, everything was
done on labels, which were printed
in-house and cut by hand by the
designers at Pomeroy Dakota. They
were then applied to various colored
paper stocks.

"A successful identity system
accurately translates the client's
personality to a two-dimensional
form," says Strohl.

> "As once told by my scout-
> master when I was young,
> 'Improvise.' This means
> taking assessment of your
> possibilities and making
> the best decision."
>
> ERIC J. STROHL

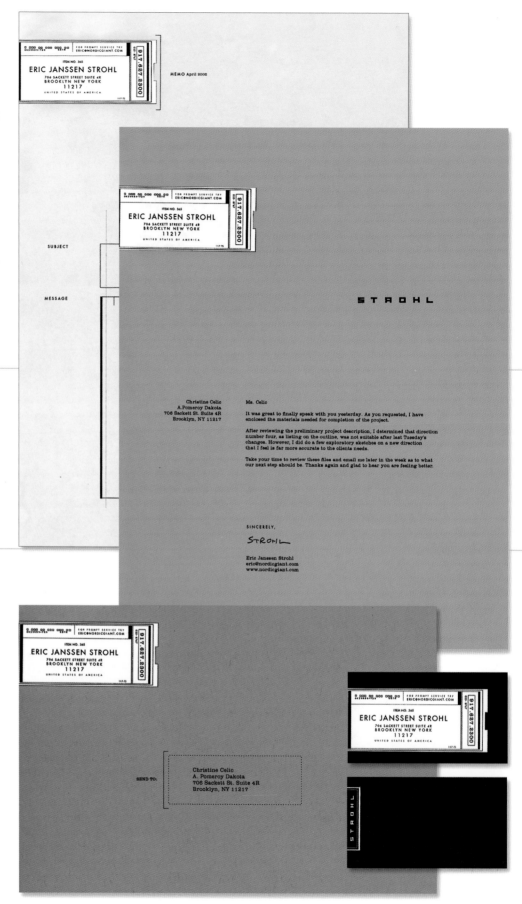

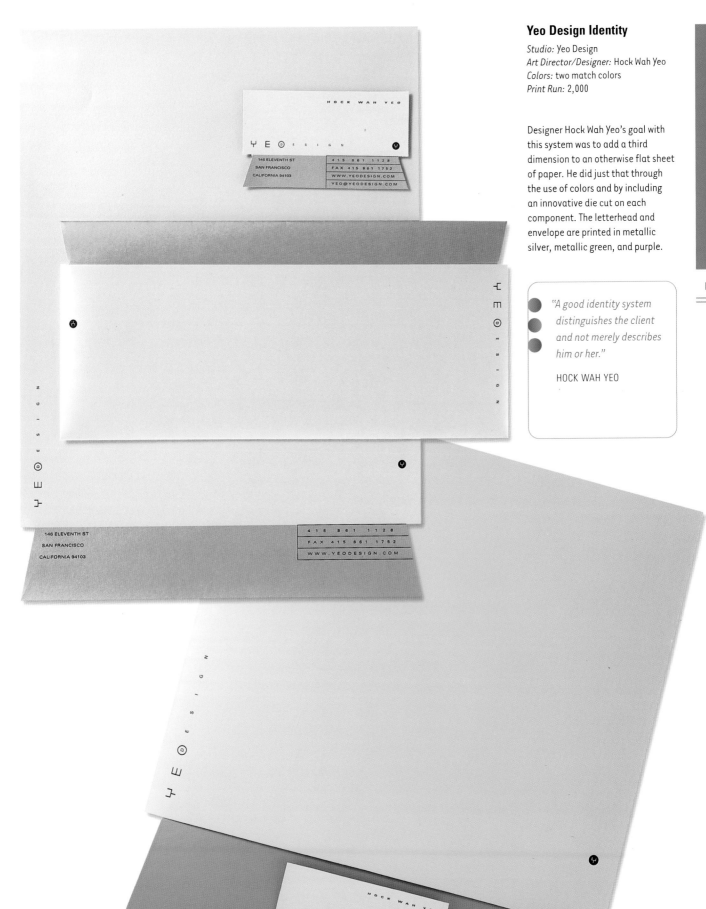

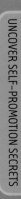

Yeo Design Identity

Studio: Yeo Design
Art Director/Designer: Hock Wah Yeo
Colors: two match colors
Print Run: 2,000

Designer Hock Wah Yeo's goal with this system was to add a third dimension to an otherwise flat sheet of paper. He did just that through the use of colors and by including an innovative die cut on each component. The letterhead and envelope are printed in metallic silver, metallic green, and purple.

pg. 133

"A good identity system distinguishes the client and not merely describes him or her."

HOCK WAH YEO

Olive Identity

Studio: Olive
Art Director/Designer: Stephen Fritz
Paper: Neenah Classic Crest Tarragon
Colors: three match colors
Special Technique: Back of business
 cards have varnish run of logo

Designers at Olive, an Internet marketing and web design firm, felt it would be too easy and too clichéd to overemphasize the theme of an olive, so they opted for subtlety instead. "The main thing was to create a mood. The word 'olive' is very evocative and enigmatic for a design firm," says Stephen Fritz, art director. "We wanted the system to convey style, approachability and a bit of ambiguity."

 Fritz chose an olive-toned paper stock and printed the job using an olive ink and a bit of red which highlights the dash of pimento in the negative space of the *O.*

 "An identity system should be recognizable regardless of whether you can read the brand name—not because it's illegible, but because it is seen too fast, etc. It creates a language of subtleties that unmistakably represent that brand."

 STEPHEN FRITZ

Plus Three Identity

Studio: Plus Three, Inc.
Designers: Megan Fentzloff, Eileen Hannigan
Paper: Cougar Opaque White
Colors: four-color process

Stickers and an embossed logo separate this package from the competition. Three embossed dots of different colors pop on the white sheet. Then to add another dash of color, designers printed a series of three different rectangular colored labels; when added to the sheet, they allow for a variety of color schemes without breaking the already limited budget. The result

is a streamlined design with a minimalist appearance that is far from cluttered.

"Plus Three's stationery works because it visually captures the essence of our studio. We had to create a logo and stationery that exuded strength and longevity," says Megan Fentzloff, partner/designer.

"We believe in taking the time to know our clients and understand their specific needs. Getting to know your clients and building a relationship with them is essential. Once you have built trust, they will be more inclined to listen to new and innovative ideas."

MEGAN FENTZLOFF

PMcD Identity

Studio: PMcD
Art Director: Patrick McDonough
Designers: Steve Tozzi, Michael Grana
Paper: letterhead/envelopes—Mohawk
 Superfine Smooth Ultra White 80
 lb. and 70 lb.; *business cards*—
 Centura Dull 120 lb. cover; *labels*—
 Fasson coated pressure sensitive
Colors: letterhead—two match colors;
 envelopes—one match color; *busi-*
 ness cards—four-color process;
 labels—four-color process
Print Run: letterhead—10,000;
 envelopes—7,500; *business cards*—
 7,500 (17 different images);
 labels—2500
Cost Per Unit: letterhead/envelopes—
 $.17; *business cards*—$.63;
 labels—.95/sheet
Special Technique: Ran two off-line
 varnishes separately to achieve
 desired effect

Vintage seals and stickers provided
the inspiration for this identity
system, which is colorful and distinctive. So distinctive, in fact, that
the business cards are more akin to
a collection of trading cards than
components of a business communication system. The quirky images are
printed four-color process on the
actual business card stock, but they
also are printed separately as labels
so they can be used to customize
other elements in the system, such
as the firm's capabilities brochure.

TIP

Labels are cost-efficient.
Printed in color, labels can
be applied to a one-color
letterhead or envelope to
give the impression of a
four or more color print
job. Also, labels printed on
a single press run can be
used on more than just
letterhead. Use them on
presentation folders,
videotapes, CD-ROMs and
packaging.

Permissions

Directory of Design Firms

AdamsMorioka
www.adamsmorioka.com

Alan Brooks Design Inc.
www.alanbrooks.com

Amoeba Corp.
www.amoebacorp.com

Archrival
www.archrival.com

Aurora Design
www.auroradesignonline.com

BBK Studio
www.bbkstudio.com

Barbara Brown Marketing & Design
www.bbmd-inc.com

Belyea
www.belyea.com

Blok Design
blokdesign@earthlink.net

Brady Communications
www.bradycommunications.com

Cahan & Associates
www.cahanassociates.com

Catapult Strategic Design
www.catapultu.com

Cave Images
www.caveimages.com

CFX Creative
www.cfxcreative.com

Chen Design Associates
www.chendesign.com

The Chopping Block, Inc.
www.choppingblock.com

Clean Slate
www.cleanslatedesign.com

Dennard, Lacey & Associates
www.dennardlacey.com

Digital Slant
www.digitalslant.com

Digital Soup
www.digitalsoup.com

Dotzero Design
www.dotzerodesign.com

Époxy Communication inc.
www.epoxy.ca

4th Revolution
www.4threvolution.com

Fuszion Collaborative
www.fuszion.com

Gateway Arts
www.gatewayarts.com

Graphics Factory
www.graphicsfactorytm.com

Greteman Group
www.gretemangroup.com

Gunnar Swanson Design Office
www.gunnarswanson.com

[i]e design, Los Angeles
www.iedesign.net

Iridium, a design agency
www.iridium192.com

Jeff Fisher LogoMotives
www.jfisherlogomotives.com

John Korinko Design
www.korinkodesign.com

Jones Design Group, Inc.
www.jonesdesign.com

K. Kargl Graphic Design
kwkargl@who.rr.com

Karacters Design Group
www.karacters.com

Ken Rabe, Graphic Designer
krabe@nyc.rr.com

Kinetik, Inc.
www.kinetikcom.com

Know Name Design
www.knownamedesign.com

Lead Dog Digital
www.ldd.com

Leapfrog Marketing
www.leapfrogmktg.com

Lloyds Graphic Design and Communication
lloydgraphics@xtra.co.nz

Lodge Design Co.
www.lodgedesign.com

Matt Swenson Design & Marketing
matts@speakeasy.org

McArtor Design
www.mcartordesign.com

Michael Lotenero Illustration and Design
www.lotenero.com

Mimmo Design
wwgkle@earthlink.net

Mindspin Studio
www.mindspinstudio.com

Monster Design
www.monsterinvasion.com

Morris Creative, Inc.
www.thinkfeelwork.com

NBBJ Graphic Design
www.nbbj.com

Norman Design
www.normaninc.com

Olive
www.olivemedia.com

160 over 90
www.160over90.com

Osborn
www.osborn320.com

Pacifico
www.pacifico.com

Parker White
www.parkerwhite.com

Platinum Design, Inc.
www.platinum-design.com

Plus Three, Inc.
www.plusthreedesign.com

PMcD Design
www.pmcddesign.com

Pomeroy Dakota
www.pomeroydakota.com

Real Art Design Group, Inc.
www.realartusa.com

Sagmeister Inc.
ssagmeiste@aol.com

Sayles Graphic Design
www.saylesdesign.com

Segura Inc.
www.segura-inc.com

SDZYNE
sdzyne@earthlink.net

Shelby Designs & Illustrates
www.shelbydesigns.com

Sleeping Dragon Graphics, LLC
www.sleepingdragongraphics.com

Sommese Design
Lxs14@psu.edu

Structure Communications Group, LLC
www.structuredesign.com

Sunspots Creative, Inc.
www.sunspotscreative.com

Super Natural Design
www.supernaturaldesign.com

Terry Marks Design
www.tmarksdesign.com

Thumbnail Creative Group
www.thumbnailcreative.com

Toolbox Creative
mary@thull.com

VWA Group
www.vwagroup.com

Visual Dialogue
www.visualdialogue.com

Wallop Design Group
www.wallopdesign.com

Willoughby Design Group
www.willoughbydesign.com

Wowhouse Creative
www.wowhousecreative.com

X Design Company
www.xdesignco.com

Yeo Design
www.yeodesign.com

Zn30 Creative
zarecki@mac.com

Index of Design Firms

Index of Clients

Note: Design firms with self promotions or self-promotion business cards are not included in this list as clients.

More advice, ideas and inspiration from

HOW Design Books!

These books and other fine HOW Design titles are available from your local bookstore, online supplier or by calling 1-800-448-0915.

Inspiration is key to your success as a designer. It makes you more creative, energetic and competitive. Unfortunately, inspiration doesn't always come when and where you want it. *Idea Revolution* includes 120 activities, exercises and anecdotes that will jolt you, your colleagues and your clients back to creative life. You'll find unique, motivational solutions to virtually every graphic challenge.

ISBN 1-58180-332-X, paperback, 160 pages, #32300-K

Graphically Speaking breaks down designer-client dialogue into something both parties can understand. It details 31 buzzwords (such as "innovative" or "kinetic") related to the most-requested design styles. Each entry is defined both literally and graphically with designer commentary and visual reference materials, ensuring clear designer-client communication every time!

ISBN 1-58180-291-9, hardcover, 240 pages, #32168-K

Inside this pocket-sized powerhouse you'll discover thousands of ideas for graphic effects and type treatments—via hundreds of prompts designed to stimulate and expand your creative thinking. Use *Idea Index* to brainstorm ideas, explore different approaches to your work and stir up some creative genius when you need it most.

ISBN 1-58180-046-0, paperback w/vinyl cover, 312 pages, #31635-K

Break through design dilemmas to create eye-catching layouts with ease. Inside you'll find hundreds of visual and written idea generators for bold graphics and creative solutions, no matter what your layout challenge. Consider it your secret weapon for designing stunning brochures, ads, web pages, stationery, posters, flyers and more.

ISBN 1-58180-146-7, paperback w/vinyl cover, 312 pages, #31892-K

From menu layouts and billboards to video packages and hang tags, this book ensures that you've got the tools and resources you need to handle every oddball, unexpected assignment with confidence and skill. You'll find formats, guidelines, quick fixes, gritty solutions and more!

ISBN 1-58180-120-3, paperback w/flaps, 192 pages

pg.143

Every design succeeds or fails on the strength of a few elements: research, typography, contrast, layout, grid systems, identity design and critique & analysis. Allison Goodman provides clear instructions, anecdotes and examples that enable you to master these essentials and create dynamic, effective work that keeps your clients coming back for more.

ISBN 1-58180-124-6, paperback w/flaps, 128 pages, #31967-K

There's no point to building a site that users only visit once. Keep them coming back again and again with a design that meets their needs, easily and efficiently with style! Ilise Benun shows you how to define your audience, then design—or makeover—a site just for them. Includes 25 case studies and six different audience profiles!

ISBN 1-58180-301-X, paperback w/flaps, 144 pages, #32237-K

Designer's Survival Manual makes producing top-flight work on deadline and capitalizing on new opportunities easy. It provides the insider advice you need to build successful working relationships with writers, illustrators, photographers, printers, web technicians and more. You'll save time. You'll save money. And you'll get the job done right, every time.

ISBN 1-58180-125-4, hardcover, 192 pages, #31954-K

HOW Do YOU Measure Up?

If you'd like to be a contributor to a future HOW Design Book, please copy and fill out the form below and send it to:

Amy Schell
HOW Design Books Mailing List
4700 East Galbraith Road
Cincinnati, Ohio 45236

Or you can call Amy at 513.531.2690 x1437, email her at amy.schell@fwpubs.com, or fax her at 513.531.2686

Please put me on the HOW Design Books mailing list so I can receive calls-for-entry for future book contests.

_____
Name

_____
Studio Name

_____
Address

_____
City

_____
State

_____
Zip Code

_____
Country

_____
Phone

_____
Fax

_____
Email

_____
Web Site